Exploring MUSEUMS

Wales

Half title page

Detail from a patchwork bedcover made by James Williams, Tailor, Wrexham, 1842–52. Welsh Folk Museum, Cardiff.

Cover

Clockwise: Roman bronze ornamental plaque depicting a winged Victory bearing a trophy of arms – The Roman Legionary Museum, Caerleon; Welsh dresser – Museum of Welsh Antiquities and Art Gallery, Bangor; Ledge Board Wagon built by H. Jones, Hereford, 1895, restored by Mr Alistair Campbell – Museum of Gypsy Caravans, Pembroke; Nantgarw porcelain Ice-cream pail, decorated in London, 1818–20 – National Museum of Wales, Cardiff (Dept of Art); watercolour of Cyfarthfa Castle, *c. 1870, by Penry Williams (1800–1885) – Cyfarthfa Castle Museum, Merthyr Tudful; Mark III model, with a V6–3 litre engine, of the Gilbern, the only car ever to be built in quantity in Wales (1963–76) – Welsh Industrial and Maritime Museum, Cardiff; study of* Winifred John *by Gwen John (1876–1939) – Tenby Museum, Tenby; Painted dial from a longcase clock by Thomas Heywood of Wrexham, probably c. 1860 – Wrexham Maelor Heritage Centre, Wrexham.*
Centre: left, Underglaze blue transfer-printed plate by Dillwyn & Co, with a leopard and antelope in an Oriental setting – Glynn Vivian Art Gallery & Museum, Swansea; right, Penny of Henry I from Llantrithyd – National Museum of Wales, Cardiff (Dept of Archaeology & Numismatics).

MUSEUMS & GALLERIES COMMISSION

A MUSEUMS ASSOCIATION GUIDE

Exploring MUSEUMS

Wales

J. Geraint Jenkins

LONDON: HMSO

First published 1990
ISBN 0 11 290467 X

British Library Cataloguing in Publication Data
A CIP catalogue record for this book is available from the British Library

HMSO publications are available from:

HMSO Publications Centre
(Mail and telephone orders only)
PO Box 276, London, SW8 5DT
Telephone orders 071–873 9090
General enquiries 071–873 0011
(queuing system in operation for both numbers)

HMSO Bookshops
49 High Holborn, London, WC1V 6HB 071-873 0011 (Counter service only)
258 Broad Street, Birmingham, B1 2HE 021–643 3740
Southey House, 33 Wine Street, Bristol, BS1 2BQ (0272) 264306
9–21 Princess Street, Manchester, M60 8AS 061–834 7201
80 Chichester Street, Belfast, BT1 4JY (0232) 238451
71 Lothian Road, Edinburgh, EH3 9AZ 031–228 4181

HMSO's Accredited Agents
(see Yellow Pages)

and through good booksellers

CONTENTS

OTHER VOLUMES IN THE SERIES

London
Simon Olding (former London Museums Officer, AMSSEE)
ISBN 0 11 290465 3

South West England
Arnold Wilson (former Director of Bristol City Art Gallery)
ISBN 0 11 290469 6

North West England and the Isle of Man
David Phillips (Lecturer, Art Gallery and Museum Studies, University of Manchester)
ISBN 0 11 290473 4

The Home Counties
Geoffery Marsh, Nell Hoare and Karen Hull (former and current Museums Development Officers, AMSSEE)
ISBN 0 11 290471 8

The Midlands
Tim Schadla-Hall (Deputy Director, Leicestershire Museums, Art Galleries and Records Service)
ISBN 0 11 290466 1

East Anglia
Alf Hatton (Lecturer in Museum Studies at the University of London)
ISBN 0 11 290472 6

Southern England and the Channel Islands
Kenneth James Barton (former Director of Hampshire County Museums Service)
ISBN 0 11 290468 8

Scotland
Colin Thompson (former Director of National Galleries of Scotland and former Chairman of the Scottish Museums Council)
ISBN 0 11 290474 2

Ireland
Seán Popplewell (Executive Director, Irish Museums Trust)
ISBN 0 11 290475 0

North East England
David Fleming, (Principal Keeper of Museums, Hull City Museums and Art Galleries)
ISBN 0 11 290470 X

BUCKINGHAM PALACE

I hope that through this series of Regional Guides "Exploring Museums", you will derive great enjoyment from the fascinating world of museums and galleries; there are some two and a half thousand of them offering an immense variety and range of experiences so there is something for everyone. It is so exciting to feel the sense of exploring new areas in the world of museums and galleries. Make the most of what is on offer.

Sarah.

EDITOR'S NOTE

This volume is one of a series of eleven regional guides to museums in the British Isles. The term 'museum' is often applied to a wide variety of collections and buildings: most of the places selected for description in the *Exploring Museums* guides, however, comply as far as possible with the Museums Association's definition of a museum as 'an institution that collects, documents, preserves, exhibits and interprets material evidence and associated information for the public benefit'.

Given the sheer quantity of museums in the British Isles, the guides describe only a selection, concentrating on those places that authors considered most worthy of a visit, either because of the quality of their collections and displays, or because of the interesting or unusual nature of what they have on view. Museums in each area not described in full are listed at the back of the guides, with brief details of their collections; please note that some of these are only open by appointment. The lists include new museums that are scheduled to open in the near future.

The principal aim of this series is to describe, through words and pictures, the types of things that visitors can expect to see and do at various museums. Authors have tried to put themselves in the shoes of a general museum visitor, and present a personal rather than an official view in their descriptions. It should be noted that specific items they describe may not be on show when you visit: most museums now change their displays fairly often, and if you want to see something in particular you should check beforehand with the museum concerned. Most of the illustrations have been selected by the authors, and highlight lesser-known objects and museum activities, as well as exhibits for which particular museums are renowned. Basic information about access and facilities has been kept to a minimum, as opening times or bus routes, for example, are frequently subject to change; please check with museums before visiting for precise details of opening times, holiday closures, admission prices, and how to get there, and for information on special events and activities.

Krystyna Matyjaszkiewicz
Series Editor

The views expressed in this guide are those of the author and not necessarily those of the Museums Association.

FOREWORD

President of the Museums Association
Patrick Boylan
and the Chairman of the Museums & Galleries Commission
Brian Morris

The first volumes of *Exploring Museums* were published in Museums Year, which marked the centenary of the Museums Association. When the Association's first conference was held in York in 1889, there were already several hundred museums in Britain. Now there are some 2,300, and new ones are opening every month. They vary enormously in size and scope, from the large all-purpose museum to the small collection in a converted house. Many of the smaller museums are less well known than they should be, and it is these particularly that the books in this series seek to highlight.

Never before have museums in general been as popular as they are today. In 1989 alone they received between them something like 100 million visits (which is more than any sport or other leisure activity). They are especially attractive to young people, to the curious of all ages and to the lovers of beautiful, unusual and exciting things. There are indeed museums for every taste and interest, for every day and in every area. We are sure that these books will help many more people to discover the museums of the British Isles, to learn from them and to enjoy them.

INTRODUCTION

In recent years, with the ever increasing rate of technological and social change, a deep desire has emerged among people to preserve that which is being replaced. The last thirty years or so, in particular, have witnessed a spectacular growth in the business of preserving the past, and there has been a proliferation in these islands of museums and heritage centres, and of historic houses and preserved industrial sites open to the public.

In Wales, the degradation of the countryside, pollution, unemployment, industrial decay, the demise of the Welsh language, and the lowering of traditional values are all symptoms of the present age's rush into the uncertain future. The wholesale destruction of towns and industrial sites that characterised the 'swinging sixties' – the decade of public vandalism – brought the crisis to the attention of many people. The reactions to the destruction are well known: the establishment of statutory bodies such as the Countryside Commission, the setting up of amenity groups and preservation societies, and the conservation of parcels of the natural and cultural environment. A part of this reaction was the establishment of a large number of both public and private museums in all parts of the British Isles. Those in Wales covered the whole spectrum of Welsh life, from farming to slate quarrying, and from ornithology to military affairs. Whereas before the Second World War museums in Wales were limited to a large **National Museum** in Cardiff with a number of small, often unmanned local authority museums affiliated to it, the number of museums in Wales today has mushroomed to such an extent that a visitor could be forgiven for thinking that the entire life of the Principality is geared to providing amenities for tourists. For it is tourism, more than anything else, that has fuelled the new heritage movement. Certain parts of Wales, such as Snowdonia and south-west Wales, have a large and expanding number of establishments concerned with heritage, while others that are not tourist honeypots have until recently lacked much interpretation. In plans to expand the museum network to less 'desirable' parts of Wales, such as the **Rhondda** and **Rhymney Valleys**, it is significant that tourism is cited as the prime reason for setting up a museum, and proximity to the national motorway network is one of the main criteria for their establishment. Of course, the traditional tourist centres have had their museums for some time, to the extent that in certain fields there has been an over-provision of facilities. The slate industry in north Wales, for example, is interpreted in seven centres, so that a town like *Blaenau Ffestiniog* is now a town of tourist providers rather than slate quarrymen. The new growth points in North Wales are the numerous small maritime museums, telling the story of man's encounter with the sea: at **Porthmadog** and **Caernarfon**, *Holyhead* and *Barmouth*, *Aberdyfi* and *Nefyn*, and in other coastal settlements, the sea has provided an ideal subject for tourist-orientated interpretation. In South Wales, the coal industry once reigned supreme, but as that extractive industry reached near-obliteration the setting up of museums was proposed by many as the elixir that would bring relief to a desperate human problem. Not all proposals put forward have ended in the establishment of museums, but throughout the South Wales coalfield there are an increasing number of institutions that set out to interpret Wales' most important extractive industry.

Within recent years, too, the countryside has received the attention of numerous individuals and societies anxious to present the artefacts and domestic utensils of the past to the visiting public. Throughout the Principality there are farm museums, often associated with working farms that are open to the public, where the techniques of milking and animal feeding can be viewed by mainly urban tourists. Most of these museums present the artefacts of agriculture rather than the story of a land-bound population whose life was a constant struggle and for whom the margin between mere existence and starvation was a very narrow one indeed. In many ways the presentation of agriculture, as of slate extraction and maritime history, provides a nostalgic peepshow at a past viewed through rose-coloured spectacles. Presenting a picture of the misery and poverty of farming in upland Wales is a difficult task, and most rural museums have opted for the presentation of nostalgia for the past, setting up a 'ye olde Welsh farm kitchen' complete with dresser, Bible, cradle and a framed picture of the hymnologist, William Williams of Pantycelyn.

Although Wales has a very large and increasing number of small museums, their standards of presentation, documentation and research are often poor. Many ask no questions of the material they display, and all too frequently museums, particularly those aimed at interpreting the history of the people of Wales, are content merely to present material almost as pieces of fine art, without tracing the story and the human endeavour that brought those items into being. This is particularly true of some industrial museums and the collections of 'bygones' so commonplace today in the Welsh countryside. On the other hand, there are some excellent small museums, and it is these that the present guide seeks to highlight. The **Ceredigion Museum** at Aberystwyth, the **Tenby Museum** and the **Brecknock Museum**, for example, provide first-class interpretation of the regions they represent, while specialised museums, such as the **Lloyd George Museum** at Llanystumdwy and the **Seiont II Maritime Museum** at Caernarfon, give fascinating insights into their particular subjects.

Perhaps a country like Wales has too many small museums; as they proliferate there usually follows a desperate search for artefacts to fill the buildings, and attics and auction rooms disgorge all manner of useful lots that can be installed but that may or may not be representative of the heritage that is being presented. Many of the collections displayed to the general public are merely cabinets of curiosities that have little relevance to the lives of the people who visit them. More often than not, only small items can be collected with the result that a museum can only present an incomplete and therefore false picture of its subject.

Yet there is a vast difference between a haphazard collection and a true museum whose collections have been developed as a result of scholarly research and are presented to the public with scholarly interpretation. In Wales, until recent times, the museum provision for the Principality was dominated by the **National Museum** in Cardiff and its specialised branches in various parts of Wales. Despite this, the oldest museum establishment is the **Royal Institution of South Wales** at Swansea, founded as far back as 1835, but now, alas, in all kinds of financial trouble. The **Powysland Museum** at Welshpool was established in 1874, closely followed by the **Tenby Museum** (1878), the **Newport Museum** (1888) and the **Museum of Welsh Antiquities** in Bangor (1894). All the other museums in Wales were founded within the present century; indeed, a large number were only established after 1970. The **National Museum** still dominates the Welsh scene and, in addition to its presence in a prestigious building in the centre of Cardiff, the **Welsh Folk Museum** at St Fagans, the **Welsh Industrial and Maritime Museum** in Cardiff docks and the **Turner House** gallery at Penarth show that the national institution is of considerable importance in the capital. Outside Cardiff the National Museum operates the **Museum of the Welsh Woollen Industry** at Dre-fach Felindre and the **Graham Sutherland Gallery** at Picton Castle in Dyfed; it has an interest in a *Museum of Religious Life* at Tre'r-ddôl in Northern Ceredigion, and runs the **Welsh Slate Museum** and the **Museum of the North** at Llanberis, Gwynedd; it also runs the *Roman Legionary Museum*, Caerleon, and *Segontium Roman Fort Museum*, Caernarfon, as well as owning two ships at the **Seiont II Maritime Museum** in Caernarfon. Within the last few years, however, the local authorities in the Principality have developed their own museum services, and those provided by such counties as Gwynedd, Powys and Dyfed, and districts such as Ceredigion and Monmouth, have achieved much in a short space of time. But the most spectacular growth of all has been in the private sector, especially in the tourist areas of the Principality. There is hardly a group of historic objects, from gipsy caravans to radio sets, from musical instruments to canal barges, that will not find a home somewhere in a viewable collection. Heritage has become a very marketable commodity; perhaps romance and nostalgia have important parts to play in its presentation. Perhaps the only future that our nation has is its past, presented (not always successfully) in its growing number of museums and heritage centres.

J. Geraint Jenkins

ACKNOWLEDGEMENTS

The Museums Association is grateful to the museums described for generously lending photographs and agreeing to their reproduction herein.

Further acknowledgement is due to the following:

p. 6 (Bangor), Ynysgain Room photo © Delta Colour, Paddock Wood, Kent; p. 7, Penrhyn Castle exterior view and Great Staircase photos © *Country Life*; pp. 8–9 (Beaumaris Gaol and Courthouse), pp. 62–63 (Llanystumdwy) and pp. 84–85 (Porthmadog) photos courtesy of Gwynedd Archives and Museums Service; p. 11 (Blaenafon), Colliers at Penallta photo by James Jarche, *Daily Herald*; p. 13, Billiard Room, and Colour plate 12 (Bodelwyddan), photos by Martin Trelawny and © Bodelwyddan Castle and the National Portrait Gallery, London; p. 13 (Bodelwyddan), photo of Florence Nightingale portrait courtesy of the National Portrait Gallery; p. 14 (Bodelwyddan), photo of aquatint courtesy of The National Library of Wales, Aberystwyth; photos reproduced pp. 17–18 (Caerleon), pp. 21 and 24 (NMW) and p. 50 (Museum of the North), colour photos of Victory plaque (Caerleon) and coin (NMW) reproduced on cover, and Colour plate 1 (Caerleon) courtesy of the Dept of Archaeology and Numismatics, National Museum of Wales, Cardiff; p. 20 (Seiont II) photo by J.T. Hughes; photo of crystal, p. 22, and Colour plate 3 courtesy of the Dept of Geology, National Museum of Wales, Cardiff; other photos p. 22 courtesy of Depts of Botany and Zoology; photos reproduced p. 23 (NMW) and pp. 77–78 (Turner House), colour photo of Nantgarw pail reproduced on cover, and Colour plate 4 courtesy of the Dept of Art, National Museum of Wales, Cardiff; photos reproduced pp. 27–29 (Welsh Folk Museum), pp. 40–41 (Dre-Fach Felindre) and pp. 51–52 (Welsh Slate Museum), and Colour plates 5 and 13 courtesy of the Welsh Folk Museum, Cardiff; pp. 40–41 (Dre-Fach Felindre), photos of exterior and of calico loom by RLM Photographic; photos reproduced pp. 30–32 (WI&MM), p. 48 (Kidwelly – photo of a Rollerman, taken at Clayton Tinplate Works, Pontardulais), pp. 66–67 (Milford Haven – photos of Docks and of Steam Trawlers) and p. 83 (Pontypridd – photo of miners lamps), and colour photo of Gilbern car reproduced on the cover courtesy of the Welsh Industrial and Maritime Museum, Cardiff; p. 36 and Colour plate 11 (Penrhos Cottage), p. 44 (Haverfordwest) and p. 45 (Scolton Manor, exterior) photos by Anthony Maxwell; pp. 45–46 (Scolton Manor), photos of exhibits by David Moore; p. 47 (Kidwelly) aerial photo © and reproduced by kind permission of Mr Ron Bevan, Llanelli; p. 49 (Museum of the North), photo courtesy of National Grid, a Division of the CEGB; pp. 57–58 (Llangefni), drawings by Charles Tunnicliffe © Tunnicliffe Trustees; p. 64 (Cyfarthfa Castle), photo of exterior by Wally Waygood; p. 71 (Newport), period room photo © *South Wales Argus*; p. 77 (Pembroke), wagon photo © Brian Tarr; p. 90 (Glynn Vivian), entrance hall photo by Graham P. Matthews; photo of Oriental plate reproduced on cover (Glynn Vivian), photo by Pete Davis.

Key to Symbols Used

F Free admission

£ Admission charge

V Voluntary donation requested

☕ Restaurant/cafeteria on premises

P Car Park on premises

♿ Good access and facilities for disabled

♿ Difficult/limited access and facilities for disabled and infirm

- **W** Unstepped access via main or side door, wheelchair spaces, and adapted toilet
- **T** Adapted toilet
- **X** Flat or one-step access
- **A** Access with 2–5 steps, or split level exhibition space
- **S** Many unavoidable steps and/ or other obstacles for wheelchair users and the infirm
- **G** Provision made for guide dogs

(based on disabled access code devised by ARTSLINE (01 388 2227), the free telephone information service on the arts in Greater London for people with disabilities)

Group visits

School group visits

Workshops/holiday events/ guided tours/talks – 'phone for details

Museums shown in **bold** type in the text are described in full elsewhere in the volume; those shown in *italic* type are briefly described in the list of museums and collections at the back.

Please note that, in general, the Welsh spelling of place names has been adopted in this volume, i.e. Merthyr Tudful instead of Merthyr Tydfil, and so on.

ABERYSTWYTH

Ceredigion Museum

Terrace Road, Aberystwyth, Dyfed SY23 2AQ (0970) 617911 ext.420
Closed Sundays. F P ♿ W
🚻 & 🚻 preferably book in advance: contact Assistant Curator.

The Ceredigion Museum, which concerns itself with the history of man in the old county of Cardiganshire, opened at its current premises in 1982. Ceredigion is a district of variety: it has an extensive coastline with a long tradition of maritime activity and seafaring; broad river valleys eminently suited to animal husbandry; and rolling hills, now devoted entirely to sheep farming and forestry but in the past a centre of an important lead and silver-mining complex. The museum, one of the best local museums in Wales, has in a most successful way presented a complex and intriguing story of the local people in a simple, attractive manner.

The museum building itself is an unusual one, for it is not a purpose-built structure nor a converted town house but an old theatre that was in considerable use when Aberystwyth reigned supreme as a seaside resort. The Coliseum was not only used as a music hall and repertory theatre, and later as a cinema, but also as a conference centre and for political meetings. It was built in 1904 and operated as a place of entertainment until 1977. The problem of the Coliseum's future, occupying as it does a prime site in one of Aberystwyth's main shopping streets, was a difficult one, for no longer was it viable as a theatre or cinema. Despite its apparent unsuitability for conversion into a museum, the local authority very successfully set about the task of restoring the building and adapting it for such use; it was opened in 1982. Its attractive displays are still housed in what is easily recognisable as a theatre, with two galleries and a stage complete with backcloth and theatrical scene, all reminding the visitor that this was a true Edwardian theatre. In the conversion of the building for museum use, care was taken to do nothing that would prevent its possible future re-use as a theatre. A great deal of the attraction of the display stems from the theatrical atmosphere of the main display galleries.

As befits a local museum, the history of the most important town in the area is presented through the medium of paintings, photographs and artefacts. The Borough Charter of Aberystwyth, dated 1277, and a model of the Castle and walled town of 1320 set the scene; after this there is a long gap until plans and prints of the late 18th century show the town just as the tourists started to arrive about 1780. The expansion that followed is well illustrated and documented, and the arrival of the University College of Wales in 1874 brought further prosperity to the town. Aberystwyth enjoyed many golden eras: as the principal herring fishing port of the middle ages; as a centre of the lead and silver-mining industry, with a mint established at Aberystwyth Castle in 1637; and as a port with world-wide connections. That exciting story of the town is well presented in the museum's collections.

The most important industry in Ceredigion was of course agriculture, and animal and crop husbandry is given pride of place in the exhibition. The processes of preparing the land for crop growing are shown in detail and, as befits an area where animal husbandry was of prime importance, the work in the dairy – butter making and cheese making – is explored in some detail.

In a series of cubicles, a number of life-like reconstructions of cottage and workshop interiors have been erected. The traditional Cardigan cottage figures in the first of these cubicles. Such cottages were single-storey mud-walled constructions, with thatched roof, peat fire on the floor, and a lath

Interior view showing the theatre galleries

Reconstruction of a carpenter's workshop

and plaster or wicker-work chimney-hood above. With all the hearth furniture in place and a well-fitted open dresser, truckle bed, and scrubbed table and chairs, the reconstructed cottage has an air of authenticity. The valleys of Ceredigion have always been well forested, and gave rise to many crafts associated with the shaping of timber. Thus, quite rightly, one reconstructed workshop at the Ceredigion museum is devoted to the work of the country carpenter, a craftsman who was able to meet all his community's demands for wooden utensils, furniture, wheels and coffins.

The valleys of Ceredigion, too, developed into one of the most important textile manufacturing regions in Wales – a rural industry in the most rural of settings, which provided work for many of the natives of the region. That industry is well represented in the museum, and the crafts of spinning and weaving are demonstrated at regular intervals. Clog making and the production of straw baskets, which was particularly important in Ceredigion, are also shown in some detail, while a collection of locally made furniture and clocks is of considerable interest.

Rural Ceredigion was not always a backwater, and not all the pursuits of its people were associated with tilling the land and breeding animals, for the north of the old county saw the development of a very important lead and silver-mining complex. Cornish miners migrated to the area, bringing with them their own brand of Wesleyan Methodism, and villages in close proximity to Aberystwyth witnessed the equivalent of a gold rush. Through numerous artefacts, photographs and documents, together with a large model of a typical lead and silver mine, this once-important industry is well represented in the Ceredigion Museum. The visitor is able to appreciate the relevance of the remains of the hundred or so mines that dotted the north Ceredigion landscape after visiting the interpretative exhibition on the subject in the Ceredigion Museum.

Eisteddfod chair from Cardigan

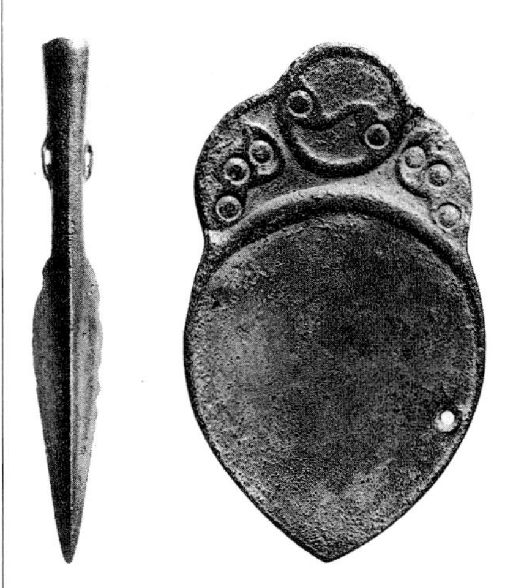

Bronze Age spearhead from Tregaron, Iron Age 'spoon' from Castell Nadolig

Ceredigion is a large area and Aberystwyth is at one end of it. Consequently, three very small branch museums at Cardigan, Lampeter and New Quay have been set up. They concentrate on matters of local interest: for example, the New Quay museum (open Mondays only) specialises in the history of the settlement that between 1830 and 1870 developed into one of the principal shipbuilding and seafaring centres of Cardigan Bay.

The Ceredigion Museum is fulfilling its task of presenting the life and personality of a region, which will encourage visitors to explore and appreciate the elements that are involved in its historical development.

The National Library of Wales

Aberystwyth, Dyfed SY23 3BU
(0970) 623816

Closed Sundays, most Bank Holidays, and first week of October. **F** to exhibition areas.

Reference material held at the Library may only be consulted by holders of readers' tickets (formal application for tickets may be made by persons aged 18 or over).

The National Library of Wales was established by Royal Charter in 1907. It was opened on its present site in 1911 but the main building was not completed until 1955.

The Library has three curatorial departments – Printed Books, Manuscripts and Records, and Pictures and Maps – and it also houses the national sound and television archive for Wales. As one of six legal deposit libraries in the United Kingdom and Ireland it has the right to claim almost all British and Irish publications, a privilege that, together with its purchases of foreign material, has enabled the Library to develop extensive collections of books and periodicals in most subject areas. The Department of Manuscripts and Records holds the main collections of Welsh manuscripts, the papers of Welsh writers and artists, a large political archive and extensive estate records. The Department of Pictures and Maps provides world-wide map coverage, including a comprehensive collection of historical and contemporary British and Welsh maps. It has extensive holdings of Welsh portraits, landscapes, topographical prints, and the major collection of photographs of Wales. Special collections held by the Library include the Hengwrt-Peniarth manuscripts, the St Asaph Cathedral Library Collection, the Sir John Williams Collection (25,000 volumes and drawings), the John Thomas Collection of old photographic negatives, and collections of 18th and 19th century watercolours by John 'Warwick' Smith, John Parker, Moses Griffith, John Ingleby, P J de Loutherbourg and other artists, and of modern art by David Jones, Kyffin Williams and others.

A permanent exhibition of some of the Library's treasures, as well as a display of the work of the Library, can be seen in the Gregynog Gallery on the first floor, south wing, and in the gal-

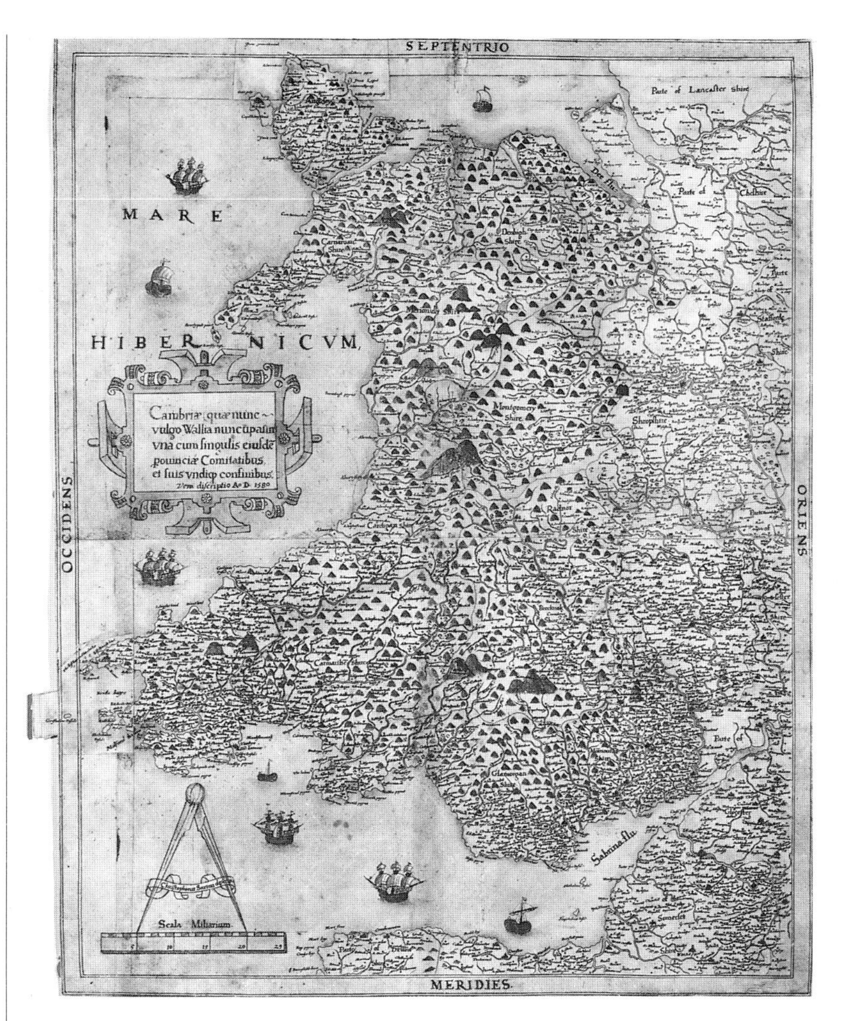

Proof map of Wales by Christopher Saxton, c. 1580

Medieval Welsh manuscript

John Petts, The Deacons *(cellulose enamel), 1950*

lery above the Entrance Hall. There is also a regular programme of other special or travelling exhibitions shown here. The former draw on the rich and varied holdings of the Library, but also include loans from other collections from time to time. Recent special exhibitions have included 'The Bible in Wales', 'Recent Valuable Accessions', 'The World of Welsh Books', and 'Wales and Australia'. Among those planned for 1990 are 'John Roberts: Portraits', 'Hugh Hughes 1790–1863', and 'Dolbadarn Castle' (see **Museum of the North**, Llanberis); the programme for 1991 will include 'The Artist's Journey Through North Wales' (shown in 1989 at **Bodelwyddan**), 'Gladys Vasey', 'Railways in Wales (Gwyn Briwnant-Jones, Railway Plans)', and 'The Ordnance Survey 1791–1991'. In addition, smaller displays are located in the Entrance Hall.

J. 'Warwick' Smith, Near Tan y Bwlch, Aberystwyth, *1792*

BANGOR

Museum of Welsh Antiquities and Art Gallery

Ffordd Gwynedd, Bangor, Gwynedd LL57 1DT (0248) 353368
Closed Sundays and Mondays. F
S: wheelchair access to ground floor only.
& preferably book in advance.

Since its early days the University College of North Wales has maintained a museum embracing the geology, natural history, archaeology and folk life of North Wales. Established in 1894, the Bangor Museum is amongst the earliest in Wales and when, during the first decade of the 20th century, a National Museum for Wales was being proposed, the College put forward Bangor as the ideal location for such an institution. The plan was not adopted, but in 1911 a museum was opened within the new main building of the University College. In the 1920s and '30s the collections were expanded considerably, and the science collections housed separately in the relevant departments in new buildings. The College acquired an adjacent school in 1939 and adapted it as a museum. In 1941 the old Bangor City Museum was disbanded, and the Bangor City Council transferred its collections to the College Museum. Then in 1973 the Museum of Welsh Antiquities, as it was by then known, was moved to the old Canonry in the city centre; it now occupies two floors of that building, above an art gallery (Oriel Bangor) that itself was founded in 1963. In the present financial climate, the future of the museum and art gallery as an integral part of the University College of North Wales is not at all secure, and the grants from the Arts Council that have been available in the past are due to be phased out or at least diminished. In fact, the museum is scheduled to close in 1990 if no funds become available from other sources. Yet the collections are valuable, and the museum provides a museum service, albeit a trifle old-fashioned, in a region that does not possess too many facilities.

19th century costume dolls

Exterior view of the museum building

The old Canonry, which houses the museum, is a listed building designed by Gilbert Scott when he planned the restoration of the nearby Cathedral in the 1870s and 1880s. It is a free-standing four-storeyed structure, with the museum occupying the first and second floors.

The first floor of the building accommodates a local history collection in the 'Bangor Room', where the history of the city, and in particular its ecclesiastical and academic history, is interpreted through artefacts, paintings and photographs. 'The Ynysgain Room' contains furniture that was donated to the college by a gentry family who occupied a substantial house in the Criccieth area. It is an interesting collection, in that it represents the taste of one Welsh family from the 17th to the mid-19th century, and although much of the furniture is of local Welsh manufacture there are also items of continental origin. The Welsh Kitchen is a complete contrast to the luxury of an aristocrat's possessions, but like so many other 'Welsh Kitchens' in museums in the Principality it is based on conjecture rather than reality; at least all the contents are from the North Wales area. The adjacent

The Ynysgain Room, with furniture mainly of Welsh manufacture

'furniture rooms' contain a miscellany of items ranging from a splendid three-piece cupboard (*cwpwrdd tridarn*) dated '1555' to Thomas Telford's padded chair, said to have been used by the great engineer when he resided in Bangor.

The second floor contains the collections of archaeological material ranging in date from Prehistoric to Medieval, and including local Graig Lwyd stone artefacts, and replicas of the famous finds from Llyn Cerrig Bach and of the Bangor Anglo-Saxon silver hoard, the originals of which are housed in the **National Museum of Wales**. Other rooms house collections of costumes and textiles, pottery, prints of local scenes and personalities, bank notes, military and other badges, and a variety of artefacts, valuable and curious, that inevitably find their way into an old-established museum such as the Museum of Welsh Antiquities.

The museum's collection of agricultural tools is an extensive one, and is accommodated in a coach-house adjacent to the Canonry. Here the tools of tillage, animal husbandry and dairying reflect the importance of North Wales as an area of agricultural smallholdings characterised by simple and inexpensive equipment. The local handcrafts are also well represented among the exhibits, although they are not interpreted in any way. One case, for example, contains such miscellaneous items as a horn ink well, a length of Newborough marram grass rope, a horn book of the Welsh alphabet, and relics of the Tremadoc hunt – a veritable mixture indeed.

Caricature of an Anglesey squire, 1750

Penrhyn Castle

Bangor, Gwynedd LL57 4HN
(0248) 353084
Open Easter to October, daily except Tuesdays.
ST: wheelchair access to ground floor only.
& book in advance with Administrator.

Penrhyn Castle, loved by some, hated by many, is an imposing and spectacular edifice built as a neo-Norman castle by the brilliant but eccentric architect Thomas Hopper (1776–1856) for the wealthy owners of Penrhyn Slate Quarries at Bethesda. The scale of Penrhyn Castle, reflecting the wealth of the Pennant family, is somewhat overpowering, as is the interior decor and furniture. The castle, built of 'Mona marble' from Anglesey, stands, as all castles should, on rising ground overlooking the Menai Straits and the Isle of Anglesey on the one hand, and the grandeur of Snowdonia on the other. The buildings and the well-tended gardens are owned by the National Trust, but Penrhyn Castle is far more than a stately home, for not only does it contain museum collections of considerable importance, but the influence for good or evil of its original owners was of inordinate importance in the social and political history of North Wales. To many a Bethesda quarryman, Penrhyn Castle was and is a symbol of victimisation and hatred; but on the other hand the fortune of the Pennant family, who built the castle, was heavily invested in North Wales. That fortune was originally made from sugar plantations in the West Indies, but greatly expanded with the development of the massive slate quarries at Bethesda. The eccentric Penrhyn Castle, which took ten years to construct, is a symbol of the Pennant family's wealth.

As befitted such a rich family, the collection of oil paintings decorating the walls of the castle is impressive. Thomas Gainsborough, Henry Thomson, and Rembrandt, Jan Steen, Canaletto and other Dutch and Italian

Penrhyn Castle from the south west

A doll in the toy collection

masters are well represented in the collections, of which over 200 paintings, some of very large proportions, are displayed. Furniture is on a massive scale. The Slate Bed in the principal bedroom of the castle weighs over a ton and is made of massive slate slabs. The King's Bed, of elaborately-worked brass, was made at a cost of £600 for the visit of Kind Edward VII when Prince of Wales in 1894. There is an Ebony Room, with furniture of carved ebony – an unusually gloomy room – and in the Library there is a full-sized billiard table. The game of billiards only assumed its modern form around 1800, and the large table of slate, the material on which the prosperity of the Pennant family depended, is said to be amongst the first manufactured with a slate frame as well the first made by the celebrated firm of Magnus. But not all is weighty and massive: Lord Penrhyn's bedroom, for example, has Chinese 18th century wallpaper and contains Chinese and Japanese lacquer furniture and porcelain.

The Great Staircase

The gardens and outhouses, like the castle, suggest immense wealth, and include a tree planted by Queen Victoria in 1859. Rare trees and shrubs, and many unusual species of tree grow well in the mild marine climate.

The world of privilege and comfort evoked by the whole elaborate castle is echoed in an exhibition of dolls and toys displayed in a portion of the former stables. A collection of dolls was given to the Penrhyn Castle Trust in 1954 by Miss Philippa Judge, and further gifts have been made since. The dolls came from all parts of the world and the earliest date from the 17th century. Other toys on display include a rocking horse and a nursery yacht.

Although much of the display at Penrhyn Castle reflects the home life of a particularly wealthy family, the source of part of that wealth, obtained from the stark hillside, is represented by a collection of industrial railway material. The extensive quarries at Bethesda, worked since the 16th century, were expanded in the early 19th century by the Pennant family. In 1801 a tramroad, one of the first in North Wales, was laid down from the quarry to the shipping point at Port Penrhyn. The narrow-gauge railway, which finally closed in 1962, was the main artery between quarry and port. The collection of railway locomotives at Penrhyn Castle is an impressive one, and includes the 'Fire Queen', an engine used as early as 1849. Railway tracks and signs, and a collection of trucks for a variety of Gwynedd quarries, provide a fascinating view of the importance of the railway in the economic life of North Wales.

BEAUMARIS

Beaumaris Gaol and Courthouse

Steeple Lane, Beaumaris, Gwynedd
(address for correspondence:
Gwynedd Archives and Museums Service, County Offices, Caernarfon, Gwynedd LL55 1SH
(0286) 4121 ext. 2088)
Open daily May to September.
♿ S: wheelchair access to ground floor only of Gaol, difficult to Courthouse.
& book in advance for visits during winter months: contact Education Officers, Gwynedd Archives (0286) 4121 ext. 2090/2091.

Beaumaris Gaol, now operated as a branch of the Gwynedd Archives and Museums Service, was built in 1829. It is a grim reminder of the harshness of justice in Victorian Britain, and operated as a county gaol until 1878. The gaol, with its cells, punishment room, treadmill and children's nursery, represents a first-class facility for the interpretation of the theme, and the exhibition area is supported by excellent documentary material describing the history of crime and punishment in Gwynedd.

Entering the gaol through a massive door, the visitor is struck immediately by the atmosphere of gloom and foreboding. To the right of the entrance hall is the room where new prisoners were admitted, and where they would exchange their own clothing for prison clothes, and hand over their personal belongings to the prison warders.

The main entrance to the Gaol

The main workroom, where male convicts carried out such tasks as stone breaking, oakum picking, mat making or making scrubbing brushes from coconut fibre, has been restored. The profits from these tasks contributed towards the maintenance of convicts, and prisoners had to work a ten-hour day. Women prisoners, too, were expected to work – washing and laundering, mending clothes, knitting and tailoring. A notable feature of the women's workroom is the slit in the ceiling. It is said that this was to allow a rope to be attached to cradles in the room above, so that the women employed below could rock their babies' cradles without interrupting their work.

A pitch dark, sound-proof punishment cell, and a large-sized heated condemned cell are found within the building, though only two executions were ever carried out at Beaumaris Gaol. One of those was of a Richard Rowlands, publicly hanged in 1862 for the murder of his father-in-law. Rowlands always protested his innocence, and according to local tradition put a

Gaol corridor leading to the gallows

curse on the clock in the church tower opposite the scaffold; to this day that clock has not kept the right time.

One of the most interesting exhibits within the gaol is the tread wheel. Convicted criminals in Beaumaris sentenced to a term of hard labour, first-class, were either put to work on the tread wheel or to break up stones for road repairs. The tread wheel could accommodate six prisoners at a time, and operated a pump that supplied the water tanks in the roof of the gaol, and so provided the building with fresh water. The tread wheel at Beaumaris is unique, being the only one in Britain still in position.

Near Beaumaris Gaol is another building of considerable significance. This is the Courtroom, which was built in 1614 and renovated in the 19th century. It represents a unique survival of a Victorian courtroom. In the past, prisoners sentenced at the court would be taken to the gaol nearby. The Beaumaris Courthouse is also open to the public in the summer, except on the second Friday of every month when it is still used as the local magistrates court.

The Gwynedd Archives and Museums Service uses Beaumaris Gaol as a centre of active learning, and a series of worksheets and booklets have been produced for the use of school children. Tasks from oakum picking to hymn singing in the chapel are performed by visiting groups, and aspects of gaol life are re-enacted in drama lessons.

View of the Court and public gallery from the Bench

Museum of Childhood

1 Castle Street, Beaumaris, Gwynedd LL58 8AP (0248) 810448
Closed Sunday mornings. £
♿ S: wheelchair access to ground floor only.
🏫 & 👥 book in advance (0248) 712498.

Near the beautiful 13th century Castle at Beaumaris, and the most sinister Gaol, is a small private museum devoted to the toys, habits and interests of children. The museum, with collections that range from home-made folk toys to mechanical devices, covers a period of about 150 years, and the small house that accommodates the vast collection of almost 2,000 items is almost claustrophobic, and bursting at the seams. The nine rooms devoted to public exhibition are full to overflowing, so that it is difficult for the visitor to appreciate the quality and content of the material on view. But even the Aladdin's Cave approach evokes a magic picture of childhood, and takes the visitor back to his or her early years. It is, nevertheless, a collection of miscellany rather than a properly documented and classified collection of material, as one would associate with a properly-managed museum.

The story that emerges as one goes round the museum clearly shows that during the present century the home-made toy disappeared from the lives of most children, and with it disappeared the art and technique of making toys from wood, metal and paper. Such unsophisticated playthings were replaced by the commercially-produced, expensive toys that were beyond the reach of many a country child. In the period after the First World War, the manufactured toys that figure prominently in the Beaumaris museum's collection became easily available in all parts of the country. Extensive advertising and marketing ensured that mass-produced toys were known to all children, but whether families in the poorer, rural parts of Britain could ever afford them is questionable. The old, home-made playthings still persisted

The Educational Toys, Dolls and Games room

Clockwork dancer by Lehmann, c. 1900

among many families, but gradually the art of making paper boats and wooden guns, footballs from a pig's bladder and sycamore whistles declined as mass-produced and sophisticated toys flooded the market.

Within the Museum of Childhood at Beaumaris, each of the nine rooms is devoted to a particular theme. One room, for example, contains a collection of musical boxes and magic lanterns, several of which are played hourly throughout the day. Victorian marching tunes and nursery rhymes provide a fascinating and evocative programme of sound effects as a background to the extensive collection on view. Another room is full of trains, cars, toy figures and clockwork toys, while a further one presents a collection of dolls, and educational toys and games. There is an extensive collection of money boxes, all guaranteed to swallow up the donations of visitors to the museum, and there are also displays of pottery, glass, furniture, paintings, rocking horses and samplers. In addition, there are bicycles and tricycles, and even a machine from Brighton Pier.

Another Lehmann clockwork toy, c. 1900

Cast iron railway engine and tender (Lancs & Yorks Railway), Manchester, 1892

The Beaumaris Museum of Childhood is an interpretation and an expression of the mass consumerisation of the recent past, and the displays have no more to do with the Isle of Anglesey and Wales than they have with the Home Counties or Philadelphia. But a visit there is pure, unadulterated nostalgia.

BLAENAFON

Big Pit Mining Museum

Blaenafon, Gwent NP4 9XP
(0495) 790311
Open daily March to December. Phone for details January & February – may be closed due to maintenance or bad weather.
£ ☕ P
♿ W: site on 2 levels and wheelchair users need their car/minibus to move from one level to the other; underground tours for wheelchairs can only be provided by prior arrangement.
🚸 & 👥 welcome, must book in advance for underground tours as capacity limited (group organisers F for preliminary visits).

In the past, the coal-mining industry dominated the lives of the people of South Wales; coal extraction entered into the blood stream of the economic life of the Principality during the 18th century. The 'incredible world empire of South Wales coal is familiar', wrote one recent author, 'but this was something far more than a matter of coal export. South Wales capital, South Wales technology, South Wales enterprise, South Wales labour not only fertilised whole tracts of the world from Pennsylvania to the Donetz basin, they were critical factors in world economic development.' In view of the international importance of an industry that was the life blood of the economic and social welfare of South Wales, it is surprising that no attempt was made until very recent times to interpret the lives of a substantial proportion of the population of South Wales. It is only at a period when the coal-mining industry is facing almost total oblivion that attempts have been made to interpret its fascinating history and to present the unique character of its workforce. In the heyday of the industry, before the First World War, South Wales had as many as 620 working coal mines, employing 232,000 men, and producing a fifth of all the coal extracted in the United Kingdom. Today, that once vital industry employs less than 4,000 men, working in six pits, and even that low figure is likely to be eroded sooner rather than later.

Big Pit Mining Museum, located on the windswept moorland above the 200-year-old iron and coal town of Blaenafon, was established soon after the closure of the pit in 1980. It is now a tourist attraction that attempts to present the conditions of work, and the life, of generations of South Wales miners, who contributed so much to the character of the valleys of Gwent and Glamorgan. At the bottom of a 300-foot shaft, visitors, equipped with safety helmets and cap lamps, are taken on underground tours by ex-miners who spent a lifetime extracting coal from the seams of Big Pit. Pieces of mine machinery, which would in any case be difficult to remove from the bowels of the earth, are displayed, and

General view of the pit-head, looking towards Blaenafon

Dennis Lewis, Blacksmith

Colliers at Penallta Colliery, 1931

Interior view underground

underground stables, unoccupied today, remind the visitor of the importance of horse power in the coal mines of the past. Both headgear and surface buildings were left intact after the closure of the mine, and a blacksmith and mine fitters still use the workshops. The manager's office and compressor room, the canteen and pit-head baths are all preserved, but the pit-head baths now also contain a photographic exhibition, and the inevitable reconstructed miner's kitchen, in an attempt to recreate the spirit of a once vital industry.

Big Pit Museum, as the principal establishment for the interpretation of the Welsh Coal Industry, possesses a large and expanding collection of artefacts, large and small, relating to that industry. Many of the exhibits are large, and the task of conserving them is lengthy and complex. On-site preservation, desirable though it may be, involves colossal resources in terms of both finance and manpower at a time when financial resources are becoming increasingly scarce. Taking visitors on underground tours has many problems, for the institution has to fulfil all the statutory requirements of safety and health. Of necessity, Big Pit is therefore an expensive exercise.

The preservation of an industrial heritage, particularly that of an extractive industry, inevitably involves the conservation of both large and small artefacts. Collieries are large-scale complexes, with many surface buildings, widespread underground workings, and thousands of tons of engines, machines, and other equipment. The railway system that provided the means of transporting the coal from pit-head to market was vital, and at Big Pit an attempt is being made to provide railway journeys as a part of the visitors' experience. It is not possible to recreate at Big Pit the houses that accommodated the workers, the mining institutes where they met, or the shops that supplied their everyday needs – key elements in the lives of the workers and their families, and as integral to the heritage of the coal industry as the pit-head gear and winders; thus, for me, Bit Pit Mining Museum falls short of expectation. But typical miners' housing survives in Blaenafon, along with other buildings characteristic of South Wales mining towns – chapels, a co-op, an early-19th century works school – and the Blaenafon Workmen's Institute is currently undergoing restoration and is scheduled to open in 1990.

BODELWYDDAN

Bodelwyddan Castle

Bodelwyddan, Clwyd LL18 5YA
(0745) 583539/584060

Open Tuesdays to Sundays and Bank Holidays Easter to end of October; only open weekends November to Easter.

W: access to all parts except second floor of Williams Hall, which is reached by stairs (lift available to first floor).

& book in advance: contact Marketing Officer; reduced admission for groups of 20 or more.

Bodelwyddan Castle is a splendid edifice dominating the beautiful Vale of Clwyd near the cathedral city of St Asaph. Situated on the A55 dual carriageway opposite the famous 'Marble Church' at Bodelwyddan, its spectacular white walls of local limestone and its numerous towers are somewhat alien to the architectural traditions of North Wales. Undoubtedly, the earlier Tudor farmhouse, owned since the 17th century by the Williams family, fitted well into the environment, as did the Georgian mansion that replaced it. It was this Georgian house that was extended and castellated in the early 19th century by J.A. Hansom, more famous perhaps as the inventor of the Hansom safety cab than for his architectural endeavours. As the 19th century progressed more battlements and porticoes were added, so that by the end of the century a lavish though pretentious stately home had become an important landmark in north-east Wales. In 1920 the property passed to the ownership of Allied Schools and became Lowther College, a private girls school, until it closed down in 1982. In 1983 Bodelwyddan Castle was purchased by Clwyd County Council with a view to developing it as a major cultural and heritage facility for a county that did not possess too many museums. 'The County Council is committed to developing a comprehensive range of heritage facilities at the castle', says the County's Chief Executive: 'It is planned eventually to establish a major regional museum and art gallery at Bodelwyddan Castle.'

Nevertheless, the first stage in the development of the castle has had little to do with the heritage of north-east Wales itself, for in July 1988 the castle opened as a new outstation of the National Portrait Gallery, displaying portraits of prominent 19th century personalities, few of whom had any contact with the Principality. English writers and English politicians now grace the walls of this faked Welsh castle. The policy of dispersing its collections to other parts of the United Kingdom was inaugurated by the National Portrait Gallery in 1975, when its first outstation was opened in collaboration with the National Trust at Montacute House in Somerset. In 1979 a second outstation was opened at Beningbrough Hall near York, while a third was established at Gawthorpe Hall in Lancashire in 1987. All three display portraits roughly contemporary with the style of the house.

As the National Portrait Gallery's 19th century outstation, Bodelwyddan Castle now contains the most important national collection of portraits from this period on public display in the United Kingdom. Outstanding among them is a collection in the Williams Hall by the Victorian artist, George Frederic Watts, who conceived the idea of a 'Hall of Fame', a series of portraits of the great personalities of Victorian Britain.

Exterior view of Bodelwyddan Castle

While the National Portrait Gallery has provided an impressive collection of paintings, this has been matched by the quality and variety of the design scheme for the refurbished interiors. Carpets, curtains, wall coverings and stencilled designs provide a rich environment for the portraits in which minute attention has been paid to authenticity and detail. Much of the furniture on view has been loaned by the Victoria & Albert Museum, London, with other material on loan from places

William White, Florence Nightingale with her sister, Frances Parthenope, *c. 1836*

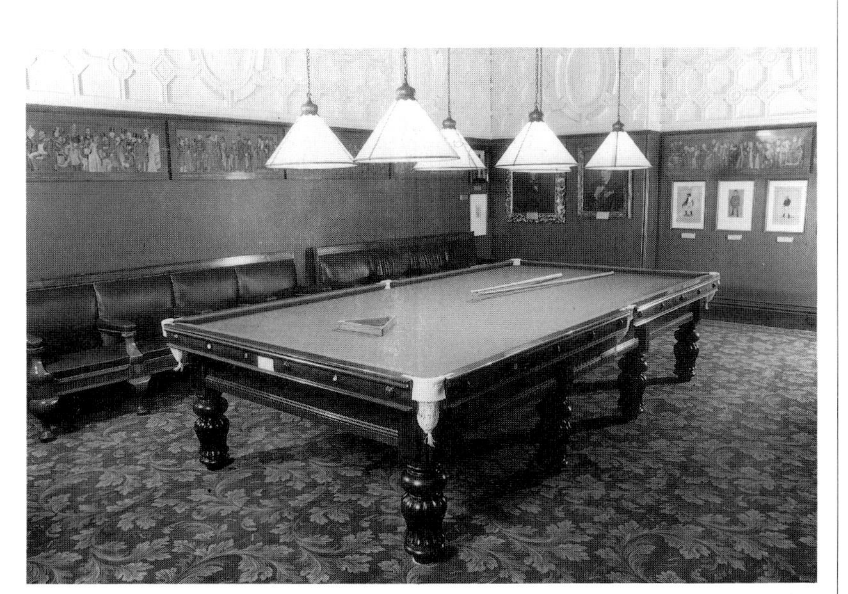

The Billiard Room, with paintings and caricatures from the National Portrait Gallery

Meeting of the Royal British Bowmen in the grounds of Erddig, coloured aquatint (detail), 1823 (from 'The Artist's Journey through North Wales' exhibition)

such as Cholmondeley Castle, Burghley House, and the National Museum of Photography, Film and Television, Bradford. Clwyd County Council itself has acquired some notable pieces of furniture to add to the displays. The Billiard Room, with an Edwardian sporting theme, is particularly impressive, while the magnificent vaulted drawing room is a sculpture gallery (colour plate 12) with three very fine marble statues on display by Conway-born, John Gibson, loaned by the Royal Academy. On the first floor, after the refurbished bedroom containing portraits of the Royal Family, the displays change from historically furnished interiors to a more conventional-style exhibition that interprets the development of 19th century portraiture. Here, too, is a small exhibition tracing the history of the National Portrait Gallery, and a room devoted to Victorian photography.

The second floor of the Williams Hall has been converted into a series of galleries for the showing of temporary exhibitions. The inaugural exhibition, 'The Artist's Journey through North Wales', featured no fewer than 140 examples of landscapes in the form of prints, drawings, oils and watercolours from the topographical collections of the **National Library of Wales.** This very fine exhibition, in which most of the pictures were on public display for the first time, was based on works by 18th century artists and provided first class documentary evidence of the images of the region's past. Moses Griffith, Thomas Rowlandson, John Parker and many other notable artists who visited north-east Wales were represented. More exhibitions organised in association with the Department of Pictures and Maps of the **National Library of Wales** are planned.

Bodelwyddan Castle was voted National Heritage's 'Museum of the Year' in 1989. Visitors to Bodelwyddan can also walk round the castle's formal gardens, which have likewise been restored and retain many original features, and round the lawns and woodland conservation area. There are play areas for children, and various events are held at weekends throughout the summer.

Clwyd County Council has plans for the future development of a major regional museum and art gallery, and it is hoped that it will look as much to the collecting of its own material relating to this fascinating part of Wales as to the display of treasures from national institutions.

BRECON

Brecknock Museum

Captain's Walk, Brecon, Powys
LD3 7DW (0874) 4121
Closed Sundays. F P ♿
🚻 & 👥 book in advance.

The Brecknock Museum, concerned with the presentation of material from the old county of Brecon, was opened on St David's Day, 1928, in an old chapel in the centre of this fascinating market town. As such, with a series of very distinguished part-time curators, the museum developed rapidly, especially under the direction of a very distinguished local historian, the late Canon J. Jones-Davies, in the 1960s. The expansion was so rapid that the old chapel in Glamorgan Street became far too small, and Canon Jones-Davies pressed for new accommodation. In the 1970s his prolonged efforts were rewarded, and the redundant Shire Hall, a splendid building erected in 1842, became the new home for the County Museum. Located in the centre of Brecon, this distinguished building, with its impressive portico, contains a preserved Assize Court, which was in constant use from 1843 until 1971. That Court is a most striking feature of the museum.

The opening of the museum in its new premises was one of the final official occasions organised by the old Breconshire County Council, and the administration of the institution passed on to the new Powys County Council, who took over responsibility for libraries and museums in the three former counties of Brecon, Radnor and Montgomery. A professional curator was appointed for the first time in 1974.

The Brecknock Museum, as its name implies, is concerned with presenting the natural and cultural history of all aspects of the old county of Brecon. It is a general museum, covering archaeology, natural history, folk life and social history, costume, furniture and decorative arts as related to Brecknock, and is very well designed.

Interior view of the Assize Court within the Shire Hall

Roman finds from Y Gaer

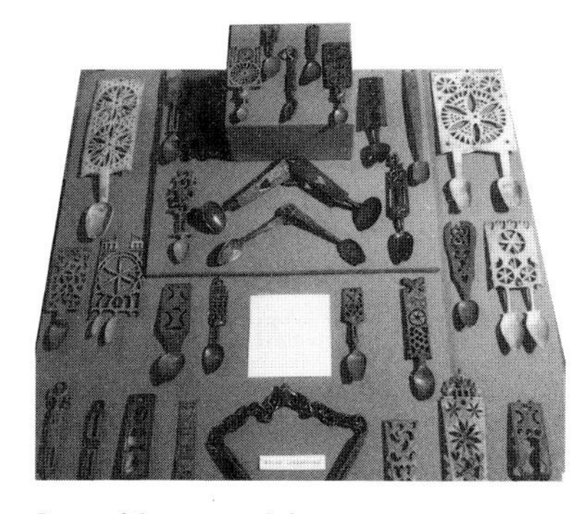

Some of the museum's love spoons

The collection of archaeological material is particularly good, for south Powys was a land well settled in prehistoric times, and the Roman occupation of the area has provided many artefacts. The most notable is the collection of items from the Roman fort, *Y Gaer*, which accommodated about a thousand Roman soldiers, two miles west of Brecon, a site that was excavated by Sir Mortimer Wheeler in 1925. This site produced gravestones and pottery, gambling counters and domestic utensils, as well as coins. The story of Brecon from the 11th century to the present is to be told in a new local history gallery, scheduled to open in 1990.

The museum's natural history collections reflect the rich animal and bird life of this mountainous area, and of the beautiful Llangorse lake. Brecknock is by tradition a very rural county, and the main occupation of its inhabitants was agriculture. Thus the collection of agricultural equipment and the domestic processes associated with the husbandry of the region figure prominently in the displays at the museum. Brecknock has a high reputation as good farming country, and the old county had the earliest active Agricultural Society, founded in 1755. The Society encouraged good husbandry, and one of its most grandiose schemes was to make the county one of the main woollen yarn producers in Britain. An active member of the Agricultural Society was the Methodist leader, Howell Harris of Trefecca, whose unique social experiment – 'The Trefecca family' – is commemorated in the *Howell Harris Museum*, Trefecca. His mixture of 'farm, labour colony, reformatory and monastery all in one' was an experiment in self-sufficiency; over 100 people and sixty crafts were represented in this mid-18th century social group.

A new art and craft gallery, housed in the former Breconshire County Council Chamber, opened in 1989. Here paintings from the museum's collection, which has a particular emphasis on local art, are shown along with costume, ceramics and furniture, as well as temporary exhibitions on various themes.

The museum's collection of love spoons is an excellent one. These highly decorated, carved spoons (see colour plate 5) were presented as tokens of love, and early ones were based on the simple lines of contemporary pewter or silver spoons. Subsequently, wood carvers displayed their skills by making the handle hollow, with four pillar-like lengths of wood at the four corners of the square section; within this hollow space, round wooden balls were carved from the core of the handle. A carved wooden chain was another skilled motif. As the 19th century progressed, the design of love spoons became increasingly complex, and all types from the simple to the over-ornate are on view at the Brecknock Museum.

An important function of a local museum is to give visitors an awareness and an appreciation of the area that the museum represents. Through its miscellaneous but well-documented collections, covering all aspects of life in the region, the Brecknock Museum is a good starting point for the exploration of a fascinating part of Wales.

BRIDGEND

South Wales Police Museum

Police Headquarters, Cowbridge Road, Bridgend, Mid Glamorgan
CF31 3SU (0656) 55555 ext. 427
Open Mondays to Fridays **by appointment only**: book in advance with Curator; total number of visitors at one time limited to 35. F P
♿ S: Museum situated in basement, access by flight of 10 steps, no lift.

Community Liaison Officer helping GCSE history students study original source material

This museum is located at Police Headquarters in Bridgend, and has existed under its present title since 1969 when the South Wales Constabulary was formed by the amalgamation of the Glamorgan Constabulary with the Cardiff, Swansea and Merthyr borough police forces. Prior to that, the collection was the property of the Glamorgan Police Museum, established in 1950 by Mr Ronald Baker, latterly the Deputy Chief Constable of the force. With his retirement in 1972, and until his death in 1985, Ronald Baker devoted a great deal of time to the museum. He obtained the services of a succession of constables on attachment to the museum, for expanding the display and supervising the increasing number of visitors. In 1986, a full-time curator was appointed.

Although small, the museum is concerned with the history of the police system from Anglo-Saxon times to the present day. There are helmet badges of the police forces of the county and boroughs, documents relating to the rates of pay, photographs showing the types of uniform and headgear used at different periods, and batons decorated in colours relating to the coats of arms of the various police forces.

Photograph taken at the opening of the second Pontypridd police station in 1868

The museum was originally formed as a means of projecting to new recruits a sense of the traditions and history of the force. Nowadays, the objective is somewhat different in that the museum is a public relations exercise aimed at the general public, and presents the history of policing in the three counties of West, South and Mid Glamorgan. Access to the museum, however, is strictly by appointment, for space within the police headquarters is limited. Nevertheless, travelling exhibitions have become an important part of the museum's activity. The first, a pictorial look at a thousand years of policing in Glamorgan from Hywel Dda to the present Chief Constable, had an extended showing in Glamorgan libraries during 1987–88.

Sgt Wallbridge, Cardiff Borough Police, receiving his brother's Crimean War medal

The collections, although overwhelmingly centred on Glamorgan material, do have items relating to other parts of the world; some of these have been given by overseas officers who have visited the Police Headquarters over the past few years. The museum has a number of exhibits relating to the Royal Canadian Mounted Police, some material associated with policing in Texas, and even material connected with the Crimean War. Most of the documents have been transferred to the Glamorgan Record Office in Cardiff.

CAERLEON

The Roman Legionary Museum

High Street, Caerleon, Gwent
NP6 1AE (0633) 423134
Closed Sunday mornings.
must book in advance with Custodian.
must book in advance with Custodian, pre-booked .

Caerleon, 'City of the Legion', stands on the right bank of the River Usk, and was known to the Romans as *Isca*. This legionary fortress was one of the three principal military bases in Roman Britain, the others being Chester (*Deva*) and York (*Eburacum*). The garrison at Caerleon was the second Augustan Legion, a body of heavy infantry of over 5,000 men, all Roman citizens, who spearheaded the final Roman advance into South Wales. Outside the walls of the legionary fortress a modest civil settlement grew in its shadow. For over 200 years the legion had its headquarters at *Isca*, but with their departure in AD 290 much of the fortress was systematically destroyed. This, together with the robbing of stones from the middle ages onwards, reduced the Roman buildings to below ground level, except for a few stretches of the fortress walls. Nevertheless, since there was little overbuilding at Caerleon, it has been possible through the efforts of eminent archaeologists to rediscover much of the plan of the stone fortress. Over the years the site has yielded a rich collection of finds, and the Legionary Museum, a branch of the **National Museum of Wales**, contains a remarkable collection of artefacts associated with the Roman legion. Here are exhibited sculptures, inscriptions, tombstones of legionaries and their families, an intriguing labyrinth mosaic, building materials, military equipment, pottery, glass (colour plate 1) and jewellery. The most spectacular of all its exhibits is a selection of eighty-eight engraved gemstones, dating from the 1st to the early 3rd century, most of which were retrieved in 1979 from the filling of a large drain beneath the Roman baths. The gemstones would originally have been set in finger rings, and served as signets, and as charms or talismans for their owners. They were the product of highly skilled craftsmen, and the gems are delicately engraved with a wide range of symbols and personifications.

The museum, renovated and extended in 1987, is as concerned in its presentation with the life of the Roman conquerors as it is with the artefacts, the construction of buildings, and the military exploits of the legion. Here, death and burial, religion, and the day-to-day life of the legionary are presented in a lively manner, and the visitor is encouraged to explore the important sites outside the museum. Caerleon is an attractive historic village, which provides a fascinating insight into the everyday life of a Roman legion.

Bronze ornamental plaque of Victory

Mosaic floor from Caerleon churchyard

Funerary sculpture from Little Bulmore

At Caerleon are the only remains of a Roman legionary barracks on view anywhere in Europe. Visitors can walk along a Roman street and discover the remains of turrets, cookhouses, bread ovens and a latrine. Each legion had within its ranks a wide range of highly skilled craftsmen, from brick and tile makers to carpenters, and from water engineers to ditch diggers: all were required in the construction of a fortress. Great quantities of timber were needed, and although the local sandstone was widely used in the construction at Caerleon, some finer stone, such as Purbeck marble from Dorset and Bath stone from the Cotswolds, was brought across some distance to decorate the more elaborate buildings.

Among these elaborate buildings, undoubtedly the showpiece of the Roman fortress were the baths, which served as the main social and leisure centre for the soldiers. The massive building, whose vaults once stood sixty feet high, was one of the largest baths in the Roman province. Discovered as recently as 1964, the Cold Hall and open-air swimming pool are now displayed under cover. Visitors are guided through what the baths would have appeared like in Roman times by artists' reconstructions, spoken commentaries and computer graphics.

The Roman amphitheatre – 'King Arthur's Round Table', according to local tradition – stands just outside the fortress walls. Designed to seat 5,000 spectators, the amphitheatre was used for colourful festivals as well as bloody spectacles, gladiatoral combat and animal baiting. Today, it continues to provide an evocative setting for theatrical events and festivals. The Ermine Street Guard, in authentically-made uniforms, are regular visitors to *Isca*. The whole village, with its numerous remains of the Roman conquest, is a lively and fascinating place, and the new Roman Legionary Museum, with its modern displays, adds considerably to the fascination.

A legionary of the Ermine Street Guard

CAERNARFON

Royal Welch Fusiliers Museum

Queen's Tower, Caernarfon Castle, Caernarfon, Gwynedd L55 5AY (0286) 673362

Closed Sunday mornings October to March. £ to Castle.
♿ S: wheelchair access difficult.
Groups & parties book in advance with CADW for reduced admission/F to Castle.

The regimental museum of the Royal Welch Fusiliers was established in Wrexham in 1955, but was transferred to the impressive Queen's Tower in Caernarfon Castle in June 1960. It occupies three large rooms, one above the other, and illustrates the history and achievements of the oldest Welsh infantry regiment.

Among the exhibits are several relating to the Battle of Alma in 1854, including medals and decorations of Sir Luke O'Connor, who won a Victoria Cross at Alma when he was a sergeant, and subsequently rose to the rank of Major General and was Colonel of the Regiment. Another of the fourteen Victoria Crosses won by members of the regiment was that awarded to Captain E.W.D. Bell, who single-handed captured a Russian gun, now on view at the museum, also at the Battle of Alma. Three tableaux show a special regimental privilege known as the 'Ceremonial Pioneers'; a scene from an officer's mess during the first decade of the present century; and a departure from the mess after the 'Eating of the Leek' ceremony, traditionally practised on St David's Day. The regimental goat also features: a goat has long been associated with the regiment and one was in action at least as far back as the Battle of Bunker Hill in 1775. An impressive collection of campaign and other medals is also on display.

One of the rooms is devoted to the history of the regiment from its forma-

Part of a display relating to the period between Waterloo and the Crimean War

The regimental goat

Officer's mitred hat of 1750

tion in 1689 to 1901. Among the most interesting exhibits are an officer's mitre cap of 1750 with the Welsh dragon at the back; the keys of Corunna, where an officer of the regiment commanded the rearguard at the evacuation of the town in 1809; and a

Some of the medals on display

valuable collection of medals relating to the Battle of Waterloo. Soldiers of the regiment wear a 'flash' of black ribbon on their collars, and the history of these ribbons is traced in a most entertaining way. The regiment saw service in the Indian Mutiny, and was involved in the relief of Lucknow; it was also associated with the United States Marine Corps in the Boxer rebellion of 1900. The display on the latter includes the original score of Sousa's march, 'The Royal Welch Fusiliers'. The uniforms of successive periods shown in the museum provide an interesting illustration of the evolution of regimental dress.

The final section of the display in the museum is centred on the history of the regiment from 1900. There are trophies and medals of campaigns in which the regiment took part during the two world wars, and relating to the regiment's involvement in Malaya, Suez, Cyprus and elsewhere. There are also Royal and other portraits of the Colonels-in-Chief by Dennis Fildes, Oswald Birley and Gerald Kelly.

Of the number of regimental museums in Wales, that at Caernarfon Castle certainly occupies the most impressive building. It is very much a regimental rather than a general military museum, and as such it has a fascinating story of heroism and achievement to present.

Seiont II Maritime Museum

Victoria Dock, Caernarfon, Gwynedd
(address for correspondence: *Eurwyn Morris, 9 High Street, Caernarfon, Gwynedd LL55 1RN*
(0286) 4693)
Open afternoons Easter to September. £ P ♿ W
& book in advance.

The town of Caernarfon, with its walls and impressive Edwardian castle, is the most important of all North Wales towns. For centuries it reigned supreme as one of the principal seaports of the once-busy Menai Straits; indeed, it was the presence of the sea that led to the construction of the castle, located as it is in a strategic position overlooking the Straits. In the 19th century Caernarfon developed into a very important slate-exporting port, and Caernarfon ships sailed world-wide transporting the slates of the Nantlle Valley in the hinterland of the port. The shipbuilding and repairing industries developed, as did a number of ancillary industries, and in due course a floating dock – the Victoria Dock – was constructed to deal with the ever-increasing trade of the port. On the quayside of that dock a small but attractive Maritime Museum was opened in 1981. The museum, occupying the unlikely premises of an old mortuary, possesses a number of artefacts relating to the history of shipping in Caernarfon, but the interpretative exhibition that traces the history of the port is a systematic one, with photographic and documentary material drawn mainly from collections in the custody of the Gwynedd Archives Service, which itself occupies a large modern building adjacent to the museum. The local Record Office probably has a larger collection of documentary material relating to the maritime heritage of Britain than any other institution, and the Archive Service's record of impressive publications is an enviable one.

Nevertheless, the main reason for setting up the maritime museum at Caernarfon was to preserve one of the last working steam dredgers, the 'Seiont II', which had spent its working life as a dredger and buoy tender in the Menai Straits. In 1980, the vessel was purchased by the **National Museum of Wales** and loaned on a permanent

The steam dredger, Seiont II, *working in Victoria Dock, Caernarfon, c. 1976*

basis to a Preservation Trust for display at Caernarfon. Since that date the vessel has been restored to full working order, and sails regularly in the Menai Straits. The 'Seiont II' is no beauty, but her restoration has been carried out with care and authenticity by the apprentices of British Shipbuilding at Birkenhead. The vessel arrived back at Caernarfon in early 1987, under her own steam and manned by mariners from North Wales.

The 'Seiont II' was built by W.J. Yarwood & Sons of Northwich in 1937, and the vessel spent its whole working life on the Menai Straits. With a tall buff-coloured 'woodbine' funnel, the 'Seiont II' was designed as a grab dredger and buoy tender serving all the buoys from Caernarfon to Puffin Island. She was manned by four or five men, and for over forty years was a part of the Caernarfon scene.

Another vessel of local interest preserved at the Victoria Dock, Caernarfon, is the diesel-engined passenger ferry, the 'Nantlys', which for many years operated a service between Bangor Pier and Beaumaris. This wooden-hulled vessel has also been restored, and sails on occasions from the Caernarfon quayside. On a more mundane level, a small locally-built rowing boat used for salmon fishing in the Menai Straits has been preserved. The 'seine' netsmen of Caernarfon have been important members of the maritime community of the town for many centuries, and the working boats, as well as the specimens preserved by the museum, may be seen at Victoria Dock.

The Seiont II Maritime Museum is an amateur effort, but members of the Trust that operates the museum, many of them being master mariners or chief engineers, are well versed in maritime lore and the history of seafaring in Gwynedd. The museum's collection of artefacts is an expanding one, and tools, navigation instruments, models, anchors and a splendid carved-oak ship's figurehead are on view. In addition to operating a museum and preserving ships, the Preservation Trust arranges an extensive programme of lectures by eminent maritime historians during the winter months.

CARDIFF

National Museum of Wales

Cathays Park, Cardiff, CF1 3NP
(0222) 397951
Closed Sunday mornings and all day Mondays. W
from Welsh counties that contribute financially through Local Education Authorities to the museum's Schools Service, book in advance with Schools Service Officer ext. 240/241. All other & book in advance with Public Services Dept. ext. 235. Some galleries may be shut during building work, 1989–94; check in advance if there is something in particular you want to see.

The main building of the National Museum of Wales is large, prestigious, and seems to have been designed specifically for a Royal opening. A dome ninety feet high rises above a marble floor; a flight of wide steps leads up to huge, brazen doors; and there are Portland stone walls: all suit the dignity of location in the centre of a capital city, and point to the fact that this is a classical temple that is awe inspiring in its majesty. 'The beauty of this great interior', wrote an observer in 1927, 'is of simple character arising out of structural necessities, fine proportions, adequate and well placed lighting and sound craftsmanship'. But beautiful and majestic though the building may be, as a functional exhibition space it leaves much to be desired. Narrow balconies around the main hall, and lofty galleries, do not lend themselves naturally to case and wall displays.

The National Museum of Wales is unique amongst the national museums and galleries of Britain in the number of disciplines that it covers in both the arts and sciences. The large edifice in Cathays Park once housed seven separate and different departments, and it still houses five of them under one roof, namely, Art, Botany, Geology, Zoology, and Archaeology and Numismatics. With the development of the **Welsh Folk Museum** in the late 1940s, the old 'folk' galleries, which were such an attraction at Cathays Park, were all transferred to St Fagans, while in the 1980s the old industry galleries, which occupied the west wing of the building, were transferred to the new **Welsh Industrial and Maritime Museum** in Cardiff Dockland. With its headquarters at Cathays Park and a network of satellites throughout Wales, the National Museum is fulfilling its role in the task of recording and interpreting the national and cultural character of Wales, 'to teach the world about Wales, and the Welsh people about the land of their fathers'. Although Wales and its people is the main concern of the institution, and the museum is primarily a repository for the heritage of Wales, it does possess collections of modern European paintings and sculpture, which have helped to earn for the museum an international reputation. It has been argued that in order to appreciate the national collection it is necessary to view it in an international context.

14th century French ivory found at Llandaff

Model of a Primrose made in the Botany Dept

Crystals of the rare copper chloride mineral Connellite from a mine near Snowdon (magnified)

With a multi-million pound building extension commencing in 1989, there is bound to be a certain amount of turmoil and disruption as the building programme proceeds. The museum, being the principal one in Wales, possesses remarkable collections, and the extension will ensure that by 1994 the National Museum will have the properly planned, purpose-built modern galleries that such an institution warrants. It was brought into being by Royal Charter as long ago as 1907, in the same year and in the same manner as its twin institution, the **National Library of Wales** at Aberystwyth. The two institutions were a manifestation of Welsh nationhood, but it was unfortunate from the museum's point of view that the foundation stone had to wait five years before it was laid, the design of the building having been chosen by open competition in 1910. With the outbreak of the First World War and the subsequent depression in the fortunes of South Wales, there were inevitable delays, and it was not until 1927 that with pomp and ceremony the building was officially opened by King George V. Wales now had a national institution, whose collections were added to as the years went by. Throughout its history there has been a constant need to present a lively and stimulating programme of

The Glanely Gallery – part of the Zoology section of the museum

special events and temporary exhibitions, together with regular up-datings of its permanent exhibition galleries. Folk life, and industrial and maritime history, have come and gone, yet there has been a continuing demand for more exhibition space, more research facilities and more conservation workshops; for the National Museum, especially since 1945, has been a rapidly developing institution with an important research function and changing public manifestation.

The institution's main purpose is to record, study and present the story of Wales from the earliest times. Welsh plants and animals, and the geological forces that gave the country its present shape and character, are illustrated in the three scientific departments, while the work and art of man is displayed in the art galleries and the archeological and numismatic galleries. In most of these rooms the approach to presentation is orthodox, with the treasures of Wales held up to view on properly lit walls and within numerous exhibition cases. Background sound effects in the permanent exhibitions are kept to a minimum; display is sober, academic and serious, with few of the frivolities you find at some institutions.

Temporary exhibitions, many of them of high quality, are an important part of the activity of the National Museum, and the art department in particular has exhibited a large number of very impressive world-wide exhibitions in addition to material from its own rich collections. The 17th century cartoons, or large sketches, said by some to have been painted by Rubens, are impressive whoever painted them, while the collection of French Impressionist works is superb, many of them originating from a remarkable Welsh family, the Davies of Gregynog, who contributed so much to the cultural life of Wales. In 1952 there was a huge bequest of 109 items under the will of Miss Gwendoline Davies, and with the death of her sister, Miss Margaret Davies, in 1964, no fewer than 156 works of art came to the National Museum. In terms of sheer quantity, this was the largest gift of pictures ever received by the museum. Among them

Vienna porcelain vase, painted by Josef Nigg in 1817

Julius Caesar Ibbetson, Caernarfon Castle, *1792*

A hunting scene from medieval life, on 14th century inlaid tiles from Neath Abbey, West Glamorgan

were works by Renoir and Monet, Cézanne and Daumier, in addition to paintings by British and Welsh artists, which reflect the taste and financial resources of a remarkable Montgomeryshire family.

The collections of applied art, especially of items produced in Wales, are extensive, in particular those of Nantgarw and Swansea porcelain (ill. on cover & colour plate 4). Porcelain was produced in Swansea by Lewis Weston Dillwyn between 1814 and 1817, and at Nantgarw by William Billingsly and Samuel Walker from 1818–20; earthenware, however, was produced at the Cambrian Pottery, Swansea, until the 1860s. In 1953 the National Museum obtained the Morton Nance collection of fine ceramics, but its holdings were greatly enhanced in 1986 with the acquisition of the collection of ceramics and earthenware put together by Elis Jenkins, a Neath schoolmaster who was the Honorary Curator of Art at the **Royal Institution of South Wales**, and an expert on the history of pottery manufacture in Swansea.

In the expansion of the museum, the art department will occupy a substantial part of the new extension so that a large proportion of the department's collections of paintings, of works by modern artists and craftsmen, and of ceramics, silver and glass will be on view, many of them for the first time in the history of the museum.

The department of archaeology and numismatics is concerned with the history of early man in Wales, and has earned an international reputation for the quality of its excavations in prehistoric, Roman and medieval sites. Its new galleries are well lit, and in a fascinating manner tell the story of early man's occupation of Wales. With its branch galleries at **Caerleon** and *Segontium* in Caernarfon, the principal emphasis in the Cathays Park galleries is on pre-Roman and medieval material. The collection of coins is large and impressive (see ill. on cover). One gallery is devoted to a display of Early Christian monuments: twenty-three stone ones, many in the form of crosses, and fourteen casts of other stones dating from the 5th century AD, which together form a considerable body of relics from the Dark Ages in Wales.

The three scientific departments are heavily orientated towards research, and important projects such as one on oil pollution and another on molluscs of the Red Sea are being pursued. The main purpose of these departments is to illustrate the rich and diverse flora and fauna of the Principality and to interpret its spectacular scenery. In the botany galleries, for example, there are plants from the seashore, the moorlands, the mountains and the isolated valleys of Wales, and in one gallery, the Glanely, there is an exploration of a piece of country from coast to mountain-peak where sounds and colour add considerably to the interpretation. Here, too, there is a display explaining the basic principles of plant identification, illustrated by wax models that constitute perhaps the finest collection of its kind in the world.

It was the geology department that brought the marvellous 'Dinosaurs from China' for the first time to Britain, and the collections of fossils (colour plate 3), rocks and minerals, together with geological maps, are extensive. The department has earned an international reputation for the quality of its scientific research.

As in all museums, visitors are only aware of the public face of the institution as illustrated in its permanent galleries and temporary exhibitions, and they rarely encounter the work that goes on behind the scenes. The collections are the heart of any museum, for they provide the basis for exhibition, research work and publications. Only a small proportion of the extensive collections of the National Museum are on view at any one time, but the reserve collections are of considerable importance, and are used extensively by scholars and by a wide range of both commercial and public bodies. Service to the public is a prime consideration in all the work of the museum. It has a duty to interpret Wales, and interpret the world to Wales, and it has to be a truly national institution.

The Welch Regiment Museum

The Black and Barbican Towers, Cardiff Castle, Cardiff, South Glamorgan CF1 2RB (0222) 29367
Open daily. to Cardiff Castle grounds (ticket gives access to The Welch Regiment Museum, the *Museum of the First Queen's Dragoon Guards*, the subterranean Roman Wall and Murals, the Norman keep and the Grounds with their Domestic and Wildfowl collection).
♿ S: no access to museum for severely disabled and wheelchair-bound, stairs very difficult for the infirm; willing to make special arrangements for blind and partially-sighted visitors, by special request.
for special admission rates book in advance with Castle Administration Officer (0222) 822081. Special facilities for student projects on request: contact the Curator (0222) 29367.

Crimean War memorabilia, with the medals and sword of the first Welshman awarded the VC

The Royal Regiment of Wales (24th/41st Foot) was formed in 1969 through the amalgamation of The South Wales Borderers (24th Regiment) and The Welch Regiment (41st/69th Regiment). The colourful and varied history of the Regiment is preserved in two museums: *The South Wales Borderers (24th Foot) and The Monmouthshire Regiment Museum* in Brecon, and The Welch Regiment Museum (41st/69th Foot) in Cardiff.

The 24th Foot is the older of the two regiments. Raised in 1689, it was under the command of the First Duke of Marlborough from 1702–1704, during which time the regiment gained its first Battle Honours. When the whole Army was given territorial titles in 1881 the 24th Regiment assumed the title of The South Wales Borderers: its Depot had been established in Brecon in 1873 as by that time the regiment was recruiting mainly from the Welsh border counties. The Volunteer Battalions of Monmouthshire, Brecknock and Radnor were affiliated to the regiment shortly afterwards. *The South Wales Borderers Museum* is housed in the old armoury building of the barracks complex at Brecon. Displays include regimental memorabilia, some 2,000 medals, and a fine collection of weapons. But of greatest interest to most visitors is the Zulu War Room, containing items relating to the Zulu War of 1879. Six Companies of the Regiment were outnumbered and overwhelmed by Zulus at Isandhlwana, and the same afternoon another Company, though vastly outnumbered, withstood attack at Rorke's Drift; nine officers and men were awarded VCs for gallantry at the two battles.

The 41st Regiment of Foot began as a Regiment of Invalids, raised in 1719 from the out-pensioners at the Royal Hospital, Chelsea (founded in 1681) at a time when there was a shortage of troops available for garrison duty in the United Kingdom and an increasing number of pensioners at the Hospital.

Items from the Battle of Waterloo

The title 'Invalids' was dropped in 1787, and the name 'The Welch Regiment of Infantry' adopted in 1831. The 69th Regiment began as a second battalion on the 24th Foot, raised in Lincolnshire in 1756 when a number of second battalions were raised on existing regiments at the time of the Seven Years War with France. The battalion was placed at the disposal of the Admiralty for service as marines, and in 1758 was redesignated the 69th Regiment of Foot. Both the 41st and 69th served all over the world in subsequent years and took part in many important campaigns. They became linked for recruiting purposes in 1873, and in 1881 joined to form two battalions of The Welch Regiment, The Royal Glamorgan Light Infantry Militia becoming the third battalion; volunteer battalions in Pembrokeshire and Glamorgan became affiliated to the regiment. During the 20th century The Welch Regiment underwent further reorganisation, culminating in its amalgamation with The South Wales Borderers in 1969.

The Welch Regiment Museum (41st/69th Foot) of the Royal Regiment of Wales in housed in the Black and Barbican Towers of Cardiff Castle and in the Portcullis Chamber that links them. Modern, attractive displays bring together a wide range of regimental memorabilia, uniforms, weapons, medals, paintings, models and regalia to relate the history of The Welch Regiment up to 1969. The displays begin on the east side of the main hall with an explanation of the raising of the 41st and 69th regiments and their early activities, both on garrison duty at home and on campaign in the West Indies. The 69th served almost wholly as marines with the British Fleet during the second half of the 18th century and their story is particularly interesting. The regiment were distributed in detachments among the ships of the Fleet. Notable sea battles they took part in include the Battle of the Saints in 1782, when the British Fleet under Hood and Rodney defeated the French, and the Battle of St Vincent in 1797, when men of the 69th aboard HMS 'Captain', flying Nelson's pennant, were among those who boarded the Spanish ship 'San Nicolas' and went on to also capture the 'San Josef', which lay alongside. As the story of The Welch Regiment unfolds, key battles in 19th and 20th century history stand out: the American War of Independence 1812–14 (the National Colour of the 4th Regiment of American Infantry, taken by the 41st Foot at Fort Detroit in 1812, is a notable exhibit; colour plate 9), Waterloo, the Burma War of 1824–26, India, the First Afghan War of 1842, the Crimean War, Egypt and Sudan in the 1880s, the Boer War, and of course the First and Second World Wars, as well as the Korean War. Various peacetime duties are also commemorated.

While at Cardiff Castle, further militaria can also be seen in the *Museum of the First Queen's Dragoon Guards*, likewise located in the Castle grounds. Uniforms and regalia of the Guards are shown here in several tableaux, which include horses and their trappings. *Cardiff Castle* itself, with highly decorative interiors and furnishings designed by William Burges (1827–81), houses the Burges Drawings Collection (which can be consulted by appointment) and displays of material belonging to Cardiff City Council relating to the civic affairs of the capital.

Welsh Folk Museum

St Fagans, Cardiff CF5 6XB
(0222) 569441
Open daily, except Sundays November to March.
 and picnic area. P W
 & book in advance with Education Officer.

The Welsh Folk Museum, one of the largest of European folk museums, is located five miles west of the centre of Cardiff. Established in 1948, its purpose is to collect and study material that illustrates the character of Wales from the point of view of human activity, and to interpret that character to the widest possible audience. As such it is a major tourist attraction, which is constantly being developed to provide a lively but authentic picture of the cultural life of the Welsh nation over the centuries. The Welsh Folk Museum has an important research function covering all aspects of Welsh cultural life, from agrarian and craft history to linguistics, folk tales to costume, and traditional music to architectural history. Its extensive collections have been developed largely as a result of scholarly research, and the aim of the museum is to present these collections to the public with scholarly interpretation. It is, above all else, a working rather than a static museum, displaying and preserving the skills, activities and traditions of the past and presenting the people of Wales, not merely their artefacts. Spiritual as well as material aspects are important: speech, drama, dance and music are as crucial to the presentation of Welsh life as the artefacts, buildings and crafts of the Principality.

Material relating to traditional Welsh life was being haphazardly collected by the **National Museum of Wales** since the early years of the 20th century, and systematically from the 1920s, but it was after 1946 that the Welsh Folk Museum was to develop spectacularly. In March 1946, the Earl of Plymouth presented his Elizabethan mansion, St Fagans Castle, and its eighteen acres of gardens and grounds to the National Museum as a centre for a national folk museum, which became established very much on Scandinavian lines. Later, more land was obtained, so that the museum today covers an area of over a hundred acres.

St Fagans Castle was built about 1580, and is a typical Elizabethan manor house occupied for many centuries by an aristocratic family, which drew its wealth from land and industrial activity in South Wales. As a museum exhibit, the castle has been refurbished to represent the interior of a typical Welsh mansion of about 1830. Of course, a folk museum has a duty to interpret the life of all classes of society, so that the elegant St Fagans Castle, surrounded by formal gardens, terraces and artificial fish ponds, presents the life of the aristocratic, land-owning families of Wales, which were of importance in the fabric of society. Elegant and expensive furniture and tapestries, paintings and floor coverings give the castle a lived-in look, while the carefully tended gardens (colour plate 13) remind the visitor that a house such as this depended on the service of a large labour force.

Sheepdog handling near Cilewent farmhouse

A considerable proportion of the museum, however, is devoted to the life of the ordinary people of Wales. Dwelling houses and public buildings, farmhouses and cottages, working mills and barns have been moved from various parts of Wales and re-erected in the museum grounds. Each building is fully furnished, and represents an aspect of the heritage of the region from which it came.

Interior of Llainfadyn cottage from Rhostryfan, Gwynedd

The following dwelling houses and farmhouses are currently on view:

Kennixton (West Glamorgan) – a yeoman's house of about 1630 from Llangennydd, Gower; reed thatched; the mortar floors of the three large ground-floor rooms were made from a formula described in Iolo Morganwg's writings. (Historian, poet and creator of myths, he was a formidable leader of Welsh cultural life, as well as being a stonemason.)

Hendre'r-ywydd Uchaf (Clwyd) – a timber-framed, black and white, late 15th century house from Llangynhafal; at least a hundred years older than any other farmhouse in the museum; the long, low building accommodated both man and animal under the same roof, and was obviously the home of a well-to-do farming family; very sparsely furnished, as it would have been in the 15th century.

Cooper, Andrew Finch, making a cask

Weaver, Gareth Wyn Jenkins, working in the Esgair Moel Woollen Mill

Y Garreg Fawr (Gwynedd) – small farmhouse from Waunfawr, near Caernarfon, with massive slate-block walls; typical of the farmsteads of north-west Wales from the 16th to the mid-18th centuries.

Cilewent (Powys) – dating from 1734 but built on the site of an older dwelling, this is a longhouse that accommodated both people and animals, and is of a type that is typical of the moorland core of Wales; the farmstead still accommodates cattle, horses and sheep, as it would have in its original setting; the peat house (for fuel storage) and sheep pens are characteristic of upland farms of this kind.

Abernodwydd (Powys) – a timber-framed farmhouse from Llangadfan, originally built in the 16th century and renovated in the 17th century; the wattle and daub walls are set on a stone sill to prevent the beams rotting.

Llainfadyn (Gwynedd) – a moorland cottage from Rhostryfan, built in 1762 of glacial boulders; one-roomed, but converted into two rooms simply by placing two cupboard beds in the sleeping end; and by resting wooden boards on the bed testers, extra sleeping accommodation was obtained in a loft.

These cottages and farmhouses (and there are more awaiting re-erection at the folk museum) represent the variety of Welsh architectural traditions. The nature of the climate, the conditions of local geology, and the availability of suitable building materials have all had their effect on determining the type of house found in a particular area. Thus, *Hendre'r-ywydd* and *Abernodwydd* represent the traditions of the Welsh border counties and the broad valleys that penetrated the heart of moorland Wales. Here, in a land where there was little building stone and the oak tree dominated the landscape, a timber-framed black and white house was characteristic. Much of Wales consists of a vast moorland with scattered homesteads, located on wind and rain-swept uplands, where it was important to have access to cattle and other farm animals at all times: *Cilewent* represents that tradition.

To add to the collection of rural dwellings, the folk museum possesses a number of other working farm buildings – three barns, a corbelled pigsty and a gorse mill, for example. But in recent years, the museum has extended its activities by exhibiting buildings that originated in urban industrialised Wales. The award-winning row of six houses from Rhyd-y-car, Merthyr Tudful, furnished to show how interiors and exteriors changed from 1800 to 1990, are of great relevance to the story of Wales; indeed, they are as relevant to the story of the people of Wales as the most isolated of farmsteads. With pigeon loft and pig-sty, roughly constructed sheds and communal bakehouse, the Rhyd-y-car cottages reflect the life of workers in what was once Wales' most important industrial town.

The presentation and practice of traditional skills is an important and expanding part of the work of the Welsh Folk Museum. The Corn Mill from Cross Inn, Dyfed, is in daily use, and the flour it produces is for sale. The Derwen Bakehouse from Aberystwyth is occupied by a family of bakers who produce bread and cakes, while the bowl turner and spoon carver produce domestic and decorative woodwork of high quality. The only working cooper left in Wales practises his trade at the folk museum, while a full-time blacksmith operates in a smithy that once stood in the centre of a remote mid-Wales hamlet. A clog-maker, producing the traditional wooden-soled footwear once so commonplace in Wales as well as the North of England, practises his particular skills, while in a corrugated-iron shed from St Clears in Dyfed a full-time working saddler produces the variety of goods that country leather workers made. It is a great pity that the large, impressive tannery from Rhaeadr in Powys cannot be in full production, but if it were, the aroma that emanates from such an establishment would discourage visitors. The

Education Officer giving a 'lesson' inside Maestir village school

folk museum has its own working pottery, which was developed around a large coal-fired kiln from the famous Ewenni Pottery, while a fully-equipped country tailor's shop is in the course of re-erection. At the Esgair Moel Woollen Mill from Powys all the skills of textile manufacture, from carding to weaving, are demonstrated.

With public buildings such as the Unitarian Chapel and the village school, both from west Wales and both in regular use, with a series of formal galleries, and with farm animals and farm activities being practised throughout the site, the Welsh Folk Museum is being developed as a major interpreter of all aspects of traditional Welsh life. The latest addition to its attractions is the development of a full-scale farming enterprise on the site. Llwyn-yr-eos farm occupies a key position near the entrance to the museum, and the refurbishment of the extensive range of buildings has recently been completed. The wide range of outhouses, from cart shed to stables and from granaries to pigsties, accommodate Welsh breeds of domesticated animals and an important and comprehensive collection of tools and implements associated with a 19th century Vale of Glamorgan farmstead. The substantial Victorian farmhouse has been restored and furnished, and in its kitchen and dairy the traditional skills of domestic life – baking, brewing, butter-making and cheese-making – are demonstrated to visitors.

A recent innovation at the Welsh Folk Museum is the celebration of festivals marking occasions of importance in the Welsh calendar. The first few days of May are the days of the traditional May Fair – a festival associated with the arrival of summer. Michaelmas is celebrated with events and demonstrations associated with the harvest, while the Christmas festival attracts large crowds to celebrate that feast in song and drama, food and drink, as well as in more spiritual presentations. In addition, on many occasions during the year, particularly in the summer, theatrical groups and musicians perform in the folk museum.

In all the museum's activities, and in its day to day life, the Welsh language is of paramount importance, for the Welsh Folk Museum is the only fully bilingual institution amongst all the museums of Wales.

Welsh Industrial and Maritime Museum

Bute Street, Cardiff CF1 6AN
(0222) 481919
Closed Sunday mornings and all day Mondays. ▣ ♿ W
▣ & ▣ book in advance with Administrative Officer.

The Welsh Industrial and Maritime Museum, a branch of the **National Museum of Wales**, is located in the heart of one of the most famous maritime districts in the world. The city of Cardiff was very much a product of the industrialisation of South Wales, and its life has inexorably been tied up with its hinterland. The three river valleys that converged on the city developed into one of the richest and most extensive coal mining and iron-producing complexes in Britain. Until the end of the 18th century Cardiff was a small, insignificant market town, which had hardly changed since Norman times. Cattle grazed on what became Cathays Park, and the Taf itself was a river well blessed with salmon and sea trout. The population of Cardiff in 1801 was no more than 1870, yet by the end of the 19th century Cardiff had expanded to such an extent that it was referred to not only as 'the metropolis of Wales' but also as 'the coal metropolis of the world'. Among contemporary writers who attempted to describe the spectacular growth of Cardiff the only parallel development they could cite was that of Chicago. The remarkable growth had one driving force: the building of the Bute Docks and the amassing of an ever-increasing fortune by the Bute family. The port attracted thousands of sailors and docksmen, businessmen and shopkeepers from all quarters of the globe, and they settled in the Butetown area, which became a bustling, flourishing commercial centre of world trade. Here too was the notorious Tiger Bay, with its mean streets, clubs, dozens of public houses, and an unenviable reputation. Indeed, Cardiff was described in 1908 as 'the most undesirable port in the United Kingdom; the dumping ground of Europe'.

In the years after the end of the First World War, but more particularly since 1945, Butetown, which had grown so rapidly between 1860 and 1914, witnessed a spectacular decline as Cardiff ceased to be the coal metropolis of the world. Dereliction became rampant, the docks themselves became almost redundant, and a malaise affected what was once a virile, vibrant community. It was in this area of dereliction that the National Museum of Wales set up its Welsh Industrial and Maritime Museum in 1977. With the recent setting up of a major initiative for the development of the area by the Cardiff Bay Development Corporation, the future of the museum on its present site is unclear, and in a few years time it could occupy another site within the Cardiff Bay area.

The main purpose of the Welsh Industrial and Maritime Museum is to collect, preserve, study and present material that illustrates the development of industry in the whole of Wales. Industrial history is concerned with man and his achievements, and not with the development of machines alone. Although machines and engines are an integral part of the permanent display within the museum at present, the institution has the task of interpreting the character and personality of industrial and maritime communities in the Principality. Wales, with its extensive, indented coastline, also has a long tradition of maritime activity. Inshore fishing, the transportation of goods and people by sea, as well as an ingrained tradition of seafaring have all been of great importance in the history of Wales. Although the present permanent exhibition in the museum, within what is called the 'Hall of Power', is largely concerned with aspects of the story of industry in Wales, it is planned that the next phase of development will be devoted entirely to a presentation of the maritime history of the Principality.

The exhibits on the two floors of the purpose-built museum building have been selected to illustrate how various industries in Wales, over a period of about 200 years, obtained power to drive a wide range of machines necessary for production. These large, immovable engines are arranged in chronological order, and range from a simple waterwheel to a steam turbine pump. Of course, in a display of this type, there can be little flexibility and the engines, although in working order, are exhibited completely out of context; like pictures in an art gallery, they are

Exterior view of the Welsh Industrial and Maritime Museum

The Bristol Channel pilot cutter, 'Kindly Light', built in 1912

200 hp triple-expansion steam engine (formerly drove a colliery ventilation fan)

held up to view, and there is little indication of their background or significance. The history of the museum has affected the type of exhibition in the first phase of its development, for it was set up as a result of public interest in industrial archaeology in the 1950s and 1960s. In 1967 the Ancient Monuments Board for Wales took the first industrial monument into care, but the Board recognised that it could not preserve a representative number of redundant engines. Accordingly, in 1967, it suggested that the National Museum of Wales set up a 'Museum of Industrial Archaeology' – the Welsh Industrial and Maritime Museum. It was felt at the time that with the ever increasing pace of de-industrialisation in Wales, the relics of industry should be collected and exhibited. However, more interpretation and the 'humanising' of the exhibits would add considerably to the non-specialist's interest in, and understanding of, what is being presented.

The Welsh Industrial and Maritime Museum occupies a four-acre site at Pier Head, and the area surrounding the museum building contains an extensive range of large equipment relating to industrial Wales. They range from a collection of buses to a railway footbridge, and from steam cranes and engines to a collection of Welsh-made motor cars. Of the last group, the most significant are the Gilbern cars (ill. on cover) produced in substantial numbers between 1960 and 1976 at a factory in Llantwit Faerdre, in Mid-Glamorgan. Three of them are on view at the museum. Another vehicle of importance is a 'mobile shop' built in 1929 for a Vale of Glamorgan grocer, for taking his wares to the remote villages and farmsteads of the Vale.

In addition to an important collection of small rowing and sailing boats that are representative of the boat builders' craft in many parts of coastal Wales, the museum possesses a number of large vessels, unfortunately exhibited in dry basins rather than in water. The 'Ivy May' was a Neath canal boat of 1934, while the 'Sea Alarm' is a steam tug of 1941, typical of the tugs that worked in the South Wales ports and plied up and down the Bristol Channel. The most elegant of the vessels is the pilot cutter 'Kindly Light', built as a fast sailing cutter for a freelance Barry pilot in 1911. In the days before the First World War it was not uncommon for a Cardiff pilot to sail as far as Land's End to meet large incoming ships, and since the money paid to the pilot depended on the size of ship, there was keen competition amongst pilots in their race to meet the cargo ships. Boats such as the 'Kindly Light' were fast, and capable of sailing in all but the worst storms.

In 1988 an exhibition relating to passenger transport by sea, 'Travelling the Waves', was opened in an historic building adjacent to the main museum building, the old passenger terminal of the P&A Campbell Steamship Co., which for years operated a pleasure steamer service in the Bristol Channel. Objects and illustrative material explore the theme of pleasure steamers and cross-channel ferries from Welsh ports, and the attempts at providing trans-Atlantic passenger services are traced in some detail. Many visitors to Cardiff are bemused by the railway-type semaphore signals that now stand isolated on the outer piers, but when one recalls that there might have been fifteen or more sailings from the Pier Head on a summer Saturday in the 1930s, one understands that these signals were vital to control the comings and goings of the various steamers.

Another important development relating to the maritime history of Wales was the purchase of a ship chandlery – Britannia Buildings – about a quarter

Full-size working replica of Trevithick's Penydarren locomotive of 1804

of a mile away from the main museum building in Bute Street. Although much of this building is now devoted to museum storage, part of it is to accommodate an exhibition relating to Cardiff Docks and Cardiff shipowners, while another part will be devoted to a recreation of a typical ship chandlery, once so important in this significant Welsh port. Premises of this type, with sail loft and bonded stores, engineering and provision stores, stables for delivery horses and cold stores for meat, were once commonplace in the great ports of Britain, and the ship chandler was amongst the most important of dock businessmen.

One of the museum's strengths is the range of material relating to the history of railways in Wales, and the most eye-catching exhibit is the working replica of Trevithick's locomotive of 1804. The epic railway journey from Merthyr Tudful to Abercynon in that year paved the way for the evolution of steam haulage on British railways. An exhibition tracing the history of Welsh railways was opened by the museum in 1986 at Bute Road Station, which is still in use. The nearby Railway Centre, a project in which the museum is heavily involved, accommodates a number of important steam engines, now being restored. Although it is early days, the Railway Centre has the potential of becoming a major attraction in the revitalised Cardiff Bay area. The station building that contains the railway gallery is itself a place of considerable historical significance, for it was from 1847 to 1862 the headquarters of Wales' most important railway company – the Taff Vale Railway Company.

CARMARTHEN

Carmarthen Museum

Abergwili, Carmarthen, Dyfed
SA31 2JG (0267) 231691
Closed Sundays. F P
♿ ST: wheelchair access to ground floor only.
🚻 & 👫 book in advance with Curator.
Nature trail, picnic site. ☺

Carmarthen Museum was opened to the public on its present site in March 1978. It was founded in 1908 by the Carmarthenshire Antiquarian Society, and for many years occupied inadequate premises in a narrow street in the market town of Carmarthen. Now administered by the Dyfed County Council, it is located in Abergwili, a village a mile or so outside the town. There it occupies a building that served as the palace for the Bishop of St David's from 1542 until 1974. The present building has changed little since it was restored and rebuilt in 1907. In the history of Wales, the Bishop's Palace at Abergwili is of con-

Entrance to Carmarthen Museum

Interior view of the Bishop's Palace chapel

siderable national significance, for it was there in 1567 that Bishop Richard Davies and the remarkable William Salesbury translated into Welsh, for the first time, the New Testament and the Book of Common Prayer. Features of the old Bishop's Palace have been preserved within the museum, the most remarkable being the chapel, and future projects include the renovation of the original sculleries and kitchens.

The main function of the museum, in addition to preserving a noteworthy building in beautiful grounds, is to present the history, culture and environment of the Carmarthen region. As well as being the county town, Carmarthen is also a very important market for an extensive agricultural hinterland. The meandering River Tywi, famous for its salmon and sea-trout fishing, flows through a prosperous valley of green pastures renowned for its dairy herds. It is only natural, therefore, that one gallery at the museum should be devoted to the history of the all-important local dairy industry. Many of the utensils shown were produced by local craftsmen; the widespread occurrence of sycamore trees, a significant element in the landscape of the Tywi Valley, led to the establishment of an important wood-turning and spoon-carving industry in some of the villages north of Carmarthen.

Of great local interest is a fragment of 'Merlin's Oak', which stood in Priory Street, Carmarthen. There are many legends associating the mythical wizard Merlin with the town, and he is said to have lived in a crystal cave on Merlin's Hill, not far from the museum. A local legend states, 'When Merlin's Tree shall tumble down; Then shall fall Carmarthen Town'. The decayed stump, which was all that remained of the tree, was removed in 1978, but the town has survived, despite the severe flooding of the Tywi during the winter of 1987–88!

A sampler made by Mary Lewis, aged 13, in 1834

The archaeological gallery houses a group of inscribed memorial stones, one commemorating Voteporix, the 6th-century King of Dyfed. It was the Roman engineers who first extensively exploited the rich gold veins of the Dolau Cothi district in the north of the county, and the most famous piece of jewellery on display in the museum is the Roman gold pendant and chain found near the gold mines.

The old county of Carmarthen was a centre of the Welsh woollen textile industry, and in the museum there is an exhibition relating to this important subject. Woollen manufacturing remained the most important of Welsh rural industries until the 1920s, and in a district such as Carmarthen it is impossible to move without meeting some evidence for its existence. Flannels and blankets, cloth and knitting yarn were sold in great quantities in Carmarthen market, and textile workers, whether they worked in factories or in their cottage homes, were vital members of the rural community.

Carmarthen Museum also possesses an extensive collection of samplers that demonstrate the skills of embroiderers in the past. At first, samplers were merely collections of stitch patterns on a piece of canvas, used as a record of stitches to be copied later. The natural development was for the stitches to be arranged in rows of patterns, and for embroidered letters, figures, houses, plants, animals and religious inscriptions to be included. The final stage was the use of the sampler as an educational task in the schools of the 19th century.

CHEPSTOW

Chepstow Museum

Gwy House, Bridge Street, Chepstow, Gwent NP6 5EZ (0291) 625981
Open March to October (closed lunchtimes and Sunday mornings).
£ (ticket gives reduced admission to other Monmouth Borough Council Museums).
♿ S: wheelchair access to ground floor only.
book in advance, reduced admission for pre-booked groups of 10 or more. book in advance; children's worksheets available.

Chepstow was once an important port, trading with all parts of the world, and Wales' principal shipbuilding centre, as well as being a bustling market town. Today's visitor could easily miss what little evidence remains of this and of the other trades and industries that once flourished here. The displays recently installed at Chepstow Museum's new premises trace the town's important past and the development of Chepstow and the surrounding area.

Founded by the Chepstow Society in 1949, the museum occupied a room above the Town Gate before being moved to the old Board School in 1968. Since 1976 it has been administered by Monmouth Borough Council, and in 1983 was relocated to Gwy House, an elegant town house built in 1796 by Warren Jane the Younger, a local apothecary, opposite Chepstow Castle. Over the years the house has been a private home, a Red Cross soldiers' convalescent home during the First World War, a school for Young Ladies, and most recently the Chepstow and District Hospital. A display in the museum describes the building's history, with small recreations to suggest the atmosphere of hospital ward, schoolroom and private house.

The main exhibition gallery contains displays on aspects of the working life of the town: the port and its trades in timber, bark, corn, and especially wine;

Exterior view of Gwy House, the late 18th century building now housing Chepstow Museum

Display on the history of Chepstow's banks

the river trade using local vessels known as trows; traditional methods of salmon fishing in the Wye and Severn, including a section of a putcher rank (used for catching salmon); shipbuilding, which flourished in particular during the First World War with the establishment of the national shipyards; engineering and bridge building; the commercial life of this market town, including banking, printing, clockmaking, shops and so on; and present day industries, such as brushmaking and tourism. Exhibits are shown in appropriate settings – a recreated wine merchant's vault, for example, or a Victorian shop front – to convey something of the atmosphere of their original context. A complementary picture of the sports and entertainments enjoyed by local people is portrayed in the adjoining gallery, with original photographs, programmes and posters.

Another gallery, newly completed, traces the development of Chepstow from the Norman period onwards, concentrating on significant buildings, bridges, and on housing, services and communication.

The museum has a fine collection of 18th to 20th century prints and drawings of the locality, and a selection is displayed in a gallery on the first floor. In addition, regularly changing exhibitions on a wide variety of subjects are shown in a room designed especially to house temporary exhibitions.

CLUNDERWEN

Penrhos Cottage

Llanycefn, Nr Maenclochog, Clunderwen, Dyfed
(enquiries to Scolton Manor Museum (043782) 328 or Castle Museum and Art Gallery, Haverfordwest (0437) 3708)
Closed Sunday mornings and all day Monday.

Of all Welsh local authority museums, this remote cottage in the Preseli foothills is the smallest. Operated as a branch of the Pembrokeshire Museum Service, Penrhos is a fully-furnished cottage that contains all the furniture usually associated with cottages from the Welsh uplands (colour plate 11). With dresser and two-piece cupboard, simple furniture and locally-made dairy equipment, Penrhos is part of the heritage of the Preseli foothills.

Penrhos is important in that it represents a vital period in Welsh agricultural history. The area around it was formerly a bleak, exposed area on a high north-south ridge that was completely unenclosed, but with the enclosure of the common land in the late 18th and early 19th centuries, some of the isolated homesteads assumed a leading role. Peasant families set up *tai un-nos* (one-night houses) on the hitherto unoccupied land. The custom was that if a house of turf was built in a single night and smoke was seen emanating from the chimney at dawn, then the occupier of that temporary dwelling had a legal right to the homestead. An axe thrown from the house marked the extent of an enclosure around the cottage. In time, the claims of the occupier were consolidated, and a stonebuilt dwelling like Penrhos Cottage was constructed to replace the temporary *tŷ un-nos*.

Exterior view of Penrhos Cottage

CRYNANT

Cefn Coed Museum

Blaenant Colliery, Crynant, Neath,
West Glamorgan SA10 8SN
(0639) 750556
Open daily April to October. £
P ♿ W
🚻 & 👥 book in advance for reduced admission and guided tour.

Part of the simulated underground mining gallery

The Dulais Valley in West Glamorgan was once the most productive anthracite-producing valley in South Wales. At Cefn Coed was the deepest anthracite mine in the world, the deepest seam being the 'Peacock', which was almost half a mile down. Working at such depths brought many problems: the build up of methane gas, roof falls and other accidents were commonplace, and the pit gained the nickname of 'Slaughterhouse' among the miners of South Wales. The pit was first sunk in 1926, and despite many difficulties operated until 1968. In the 1960s, however, as the difficulties of deep mining multiplied, much of the labour force was transferred to the adjacent Blaenant drift mine, where coal seams at a shallower depth are still operational. In no way could the Cefn Coed Colliery be opened for underground visits as with **Big Pit** at Blaenafon, but nevertheless all the key surface buildings and the machinery of the old colliery have been preserved. With its simulated underground mining gallery, the museum provides a fascinating insight into the history of South Wales' most important extractive industry. The proximity of Cefn Coed Museum to a working drift mine provides the correct and apt atmosphere for an interpretative experience.

In the boilerhouse

The most spectacular of all the exhibits at the museum are the six giant boilers, which provided the steam that powered the two winding engines and the water pumps that in later years were also to heat water for the pit-head baths. These Lancashire boilers, each with two fire tubes, were powered by coal and later by methane, but when coal was used the fire tubes needed de-scaling every two years, a filthy, thankless task. Until 1937 the boilers were in the open air and the stokers worked out of doors in all weathers, both day and night. As Albert Hockeridge writes in the excellent museum guide, 'The three stokers who kept

Morlais winding engine

these boilers going worked eight hour shifts, shovelling over two tons of coal into each working boiler during this time. It was hard work, but at least four of the boilers had to be kept working at any time, in order to power the two steam winding engines. The work of cleaning and repairing was even harder because we had to climb into a boiler while the boilers either side were still under steam. One of the perks of the boilerman's job was that he could cook himself a breakfast of bacon and eggs on a shovel in the boiler on the early shift.'

The massive winding engine for the downcast – the ventilating shaft – is the centrepiece of the Cefn Coed Museum. Manufactured in 1927 by Worsley Mesnes of Wigan, the massive engine generated 1600 horse power, and its drum held two wire ropes with a breaking strain of 234 tons. Nearby, the compressor house once supplied power for most of the equipment used in the pit. In very gassy pits such as Cefn Coed electricity was dangerous to use because of the risk of explosion from friction or static sparks. Compressed air was far safer, and was therefore used to power drills, haulage engines and pumps, as well as for lighting and ventilation. In its heyday the Cefn Coed Pit operated as many as five compressors.

The attraction of the Cefn Coed museum is the on-site preservation of the essential equipment of a coal mine. From Weir pumps used to feed water to the boilers, salvaged from a First World War battleship, to the spectacular winding engine, the museum has an air of reality and authenticity. The mining exhibition gallery, where the history of the South Wales coal industry is interpreted, tells the story of coal from its formation in the Carboniferous period, and covers the development of coal mining in the Neath and Dulais Valley in some detail. This is followed by a history of the Cefn Coed Colliery itself, from the early unsuccessful attempts to sink the pit, through success, prosperity, decline, and eventual closure. The methods of mining practised at Cefn Coed are also contrasted with the modern, mechanised coalface now being worked in the adjacent Blaenant Colliery. The continuing importance of open-cast mining, so widespread on the northern rim of the South Wales coalfield, is explored, and the small private mines of the Dulais Valley, which are still of some significance, are also illustrated. The complex at Cefn Coed very effectively reflects the history, the present situation, and the future of the South Wales coal industry, providing as it does a complete and fascinating insight into an industry that was the life-blood of South Wales. It presents a human as well as a technological story, and is in every way a tribute to a remarkable group of working men who brought prosperity to the Principality.

CYNONVILLE

Welsh Miner's Museum

Afan Argoed Country Park, Cynonville, Port Talbot, West Glamorgan SA13 3HG (0639) 850564
Open daily April to October, weekends only November to March. W
& book in advance: contact museum, or Director/Secretary (0639) 850875; pre-booked visits accepted for weekdays November to March.

They no longer mine coal in the Afan Valley, for in 1970 the last mine closed and a number of close-knit village communities found themselves with no source of livelihood. For over two centuries the high-quality coking coals of the narrow valley leading northwards from Port Talbot provided the raw material for the iron, copper and tinplate works of the region, and the whole life of villages, from Cwmafan to Glyncorrwg and Abergwynfi, revolved around the coal mines that employed most of the male residents. When coal mining in the Afan Valley ceased with the closure of the last mine at Glyncorrwg in 1970, there was despondency amongst the villagers as they had no other source of income, and the area as a whole was faced with the prospect of grave economic decline. In 1971, however, in an attempt to alleviate the condition of heavy unemployment, a Community Development Project Team was set up in conjunction with the old Glamorgan County Council to examine the problems of the area and help to foster ideas for rehabilitation. The one positive proposal that emerged was to establish a museum on the disused colliery site at Glyncorrwg. An extensive building was available, for only a few years before the closure of the mine the National Coal Board, in its wisdom, had spent £3½ million on modernising the mine, soon destined to be abandoned. Unfortunately, there were financial problems, and it was

Building the pit-head frame at Cynon Colliery, Cynonville, 1908

Tableau of a boy pushing a cart underground

Tableau, miners in return roadway underground

soon found that Glyncorrwg was not the ideal site for a major mining museum. The village lay in a cul-de-sac valley with a difficult, twisting approach, while the colliery itself was approached by a single, narrow and steep mountain road. Although an extensive collection of artefacts and reminiscences, photographs and documents had been amassed by an enthusiastic body of voluntary workers, it was obvious that the peaceful village of Glyncorrwg could not be the site for the new museum.

Fortuitously in 1972, six miles down the Afan Valley, the Glamorgan County Council and the Forestry Commission had created the beautiful Afan Argoed Country Park. It was within this park that the Welsh Miner's Museum was established, and the first stage was opened to the general public in 1975. With the hard work and dedication of local people a simulated underground gallery was prepared, complete with underground stable and pit pony. The pit gear and mining equipment on display all add up to provide an evocative picture of the harsh realities of coal cutting, and an understanding of the effect of the industry on the communities of the South Wales valleys. The Welsh Miner's Museum is important in that it was set up by members of the local community, by people with knowledge of the history and character of the mining

A horse in the underground stable

villages. At the Welsh Miner's Museum the personality of those unique communities is interpreted in a most successful and dramatic way.

The museum at Afan Argoed is not merely a technological museum exploring the techniques of mining coal, but one that explores the life of the Afan Valley. In the display, sport and recreation, the mineworkers union, child labour, pneumoconiosis and colliery disasters are all explored. The homes of the people are not forgotten, for in the terraces of the valleys the women worked as hard as the men. They baked in the blackleaded, shining grates; they boiled water for tired, blackened men coming home from different shifts to bath before the open fire; they greased their boots, scrubbed, washed, darned, sewed clothes and brought up children. The warmth and vitality of a mining community is brought out through the display of unique photographs and reconstructed homes within the Miner's Museum. An interpretation of the coal industry is never complete unless it creates an awareness of what it was like to live in a mining community, as is presented so successfully here.

DRE-FACH FELINDRE

Museum of the Welsh Woollen Industry

Dre-Fach Felindre, Llandysul, Dyfed SA44 5UP (0559) 370929
Closed Sundays all year, and Saturdays October to March. £
☕ and picnic site. P
♿ S: wheelchair access to ground floor only.
🚻 & 👥 book in advance.

The Museum of the Welsh Woollen Industry was established as a branch of the **National Museum of Wales** (Welsh Folk Museum) in 1976. It sets out to trace the history of the most extensive and important of all Welsh rural industries in the authentic location of a large, comprehensive woollen mill. The Cambrian Mills, Dre-Fach Felindre, were the largest of all the mills in a village that was until 1939 almost entirely dependent on the woollen industry. The mill buildings that accommodate the museum are typical of the large-scale enterprises that dominated the woollen industry in west Wales during its heyday between 1880 and 1925. They now contain far more than a museum that traces the history and technology of an industry, for this is a living museum that accommodates a fully-working mill, Melin Teifi, which is also open to visitors.

At Melin Teifi, geared entirely to modern production, furnishing fabrics, fashion and dress material, shirts, colourful blankets, and a wide range of modern fashion wear in light flannel are produced, most of them for the export market. Melin Teifi is an integral part of the museum, helping to show that present-day textile production in Wales is just as important as the long history of the industry. Instead of merely showing a dead, forgotten past, the museum was planned and conceived as a full interpretative facility for an important industry, and an attempt has been made to bring the story of that industry right up to date, to make its history relevant and to provide,

Exterior view of the Cambrian Mills, Dre-Fach Felindre

Weaving at the calico loom

Example of cloth woven at Melin Teifi

perhaps, a sound basis for the future. The museum aims, among other things, to act as a shop window for the woollen industry in all parts of Wales.

A considerable proportion of the museum building is devoted to the history of the Welsh woollen industry in its most important region, and as such it is closely tied to the aims of its parent, the **Welsh Folk Museum** at St Fagans. In the grounds of the Welsh Folk Museum is the Esgair Moel Woollen Mill, moved from Brecknock in 1953 and installed as a fully-working exhibit. That small mill only represented the industry at its simplest level. Mills such as the Esgair Moel were concerned with supplying a strictly local need, and a balanced representation of the industry was far from complete without the preservation of a much larger type of mill in an important textile-producing region.

A substantial section of the exhibition at the museum is devoted to the exciting, though brief, story of Dre-fach Felindre as a textile-producing centre. The character and personality of the area cannot be understood without knowing something about the industry that once employed a large section of the population. This remote village was once 'The Huddersfield of Wales', with mills located along the banks of its swiftly flowing streams. The markets for its products were people in the industrial valleys of South Wales, and the sale of flannel and tweed brought unprecedented prosperity, albeit short-lived, to the manufacturers in rural West Wales.

A 'factory trail' through the village is an important part of the experience of visiting this museum for, within a mile of it, all the evolutionary stages in the development of the textile industry, from fulling mill to weaver's cottage and from teasel garden to mill leat, may be seen. Many of the village's fifty mills are still standing, but only three are still in production.

In addition to presenting the story of Dre-fach Felindre as a centre of textile manufacturing, the earlier technical and regional history of the Welsh woollen industry is also presented. Until the mid-19th century, for example, the most important textile region in Wales was the upper Severn Valley, and there are a number of sections in the exhibition devoted to the history of the flannel trade in **Newtown, Llanidloes** and **Welshpool.**

On the ground floor of the museum a comprehensive collection of equipment relating to the development of the woollen industry is exhibited. All these items are in working order, and are demonstrated by highly skilled and experienced members of the museum staff. Carding, spinning, weaving and finishing equipment is presented in evolutionary sequences, and the collection is probably the most comprehensive in Britain. Outside the main building, a garden growing the plants that were used in cloth dyeing is being developed, while an open-sided 'windshed' for the drying of woven shawls has recently been restored, ready for use. In addition, a large building, once a weaving shed, accommodates three independent master-craftsmen making the traditional products of west Wales for sale to the public.

The whole aim of the complex at Dre-fach Felindre is to present Welsh industrial activity as a living organism, contributing not only to knowledge of the heritage of the Principality, but also to the economic welfare of a community that has suffered greatly from the unemployment of its people.

The shawl hot press

HAVERFORDWEST

Graham Sutherland Gallery

Picton Castle, The Rhos, Haverfordwest, Dyfed (043786) 296
Closed Mondays. £ P ♿ W
if booked in advance;
& book in advance if lecture required.
Access to Library by arrangement (no wheelchair access to Library).

The Graham Sutherland Gallery was established in 1976, and is situated in refurbished buildings adjacent to Picton Castle, near Haverfordwest in Dyfed. The gallery features the work of one of Britain's most distinguished artists, and the collection is based on the gift made to the nation by Sutherland and his wife of work with particular reference to the surrounding Pembrokeshire countryside, which the artist felt had given him most inspiration (colour plate 2). Sutherland believed that his paintings would be better understood in the area where he had worked. Since the artist's death in 1980 the collection has been greatly enlarged. The gallery is now an outstation of the **National Museum of Wales** and its Department of Art. The present collection, of over 500 items, includes oils, gouaches and prints, from early etchings to his last lithographs of 1979. There are portrait studies, religious studies, and designs for tapestry, as well as many studies of natural forms and landscape.

The Pembrokeshire coast was the catalyst that changed Graham Sutherland (1903–80) from an accomplished etcher into one of the giants among 20th century British artists. In 1973 he recalled the excitement that he had felt on his first visit to south-west Wales: 'From the moment I set foot in Wales, I was obsessed. I have worked there, particularly in Pembrokeshire every year since 1934; with one long regrettable gap, brought about by the fact that I thought I had exhausted what the countryside had to offer both as a 'vocabulary' and as inspiration. I was sadly mistaken and in the last ten years I made up for it, continuing my visits in order to improve my status and to soak myself in the curiously charged atmosphere – at once both calm and exciting; to meet people and to benefit on good days from the extraordinary clear and transparent light'.

Study for Thorn Tree, 1945

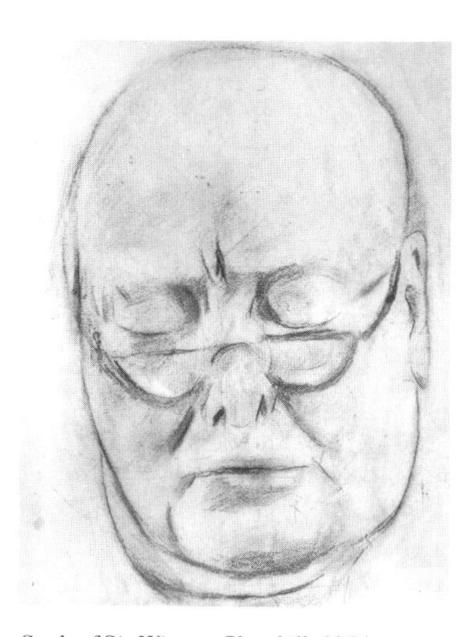

Study of Sir Winston Churchill, 1954

It was the woodland, the estuaries, and the gnarled trees, often with fantastic root-forms, that were sources of inspiration to the artist, and his striking paintings are deeply rooted in the countryside of one of Britain's most beautiful regions. Most of the works on display at the gallery were directly inspired by south-west Wales. The selection of works on display is changed regularly.

In establishing a gallery at Picton Castle, Sutherland believed that the display of his pictures near the sites that had inspired them would be a telling experience for the visitor: the countryside would act as a natural lead-in to his art, and reciprocally his pictures would sharpen the visitor's awareness and appreciation of the extraordinary character of the Pembrokeshire landscape. In the Victorian and Edwardian eras, Wales was the most frequently painted part of the British Isles, and the Principality was the inspiration for such artists as J.M.W. Turner, Richard Wilson and David Cox. Sutherland was the most outstanding of 20th century artists who fell under its spell, and for whom phenomenal creative energy was unleashed by the Welsh landscape.

In addition to the gallery containing first-class paintings, Picton Castle itself, with its gardens and extensive woodland, is a fascinating place to visit, located in the heart of a serene and beautiful countryside of gentle slopes and lush pastures.

Cathedral (Study of Rocks), 1975

Welsh Landscape, 1936 (gouache made on the road between Newgate and Little Haven, Pembrokeshire)

Haverfordwest Castle Museum & Art Gallery

The Castle, Haverfordwest, Pembrokeshire, Dyfed SA61 2EF
(0437) 3708
Closed Sundays all year, and Mondays October to May. £ P
♿ S: museum on first floor plus balcony floor, access by stairs only.
🚻 & 👥 book in advance.

Haverfordwest, the county town of the old county of Pembrokeshire, is an ancient and important town, once a port of great significance. It first rose to prominence with the arrival of the Normans, who recognised its strategic location in the heart of south-west Wales; in subsequent years Flemish settlers came, and the town grew in importance as one of the chief commercial and administrative centres of the region.

Dominating the town today are the remains of the 12th–13th century castle that occupied a strong defensive position overlooking the river Cleddau and the rolling countryside of 'Little England beyond Wales'. Within the remaining walls of the ramparts, the county gaol, which later served as the police headquarters for the old Pembrokeshire Constabulary, was built in the early 19th century. It is this somewhat stark building that accommodates the Castle Museum and Art Gallery run by the Pembrokeshire Museum Service).

Part of the maritime display

The ground floor of the building houses the Pembrokeshire section of the Dyfed Record Office, while an elegant staircase leads to the museum on the first floor, which has a miscellany of material relating to the history and art of Pembrokeshire. A part of the exhibition area is devoted to the history of the town as a regional centre of commerce and administration, while the impressive collection of military uniforms gives an insight into the military history of this western outpoint of Wales. The building of a number of castles by the Norman conquerors of Pembrokeshire is discussed, as is the long history of the area as an important front-line in the defence of the realm. It would be interesting to see more on the importance of **Milford Haven** as a naval port, and of Pembroke Dock as a pre-eminent centre for the construction of naval vessels until the 1860s – a fascinating story that is worthy of interpretation.

The building also serves as a temporary exhibition centre for the region and receives regular touring exhibitions. The gallery has a small collection of local art, with a growing print collection. In addition, it maintains an up-to-date 'Register of Pembrokeshire Artists' available to researchers and people interested in buying works by the many artists who have settled in this idyllic region.

Exterior view of Haverfordwest Castle

Scolton Manor Country Park Museum

Spittal, Haverfordwest, Dyfed
SA62 5QL (043782) 328
Open Tuesdays to Sundays May to September.
ST: wheelchair access to some parts.
& book in advance with Curator/Museum Secretary.

Scolton Manor Museum, located in a sixty-acre country park, sets out to interpret the history and natural environment of the old county of Pembrokeshire. Although the history of the manor may be traced back to the 14th century, the house itself was built in 1840 for the Higgon family, who occupied the premises continuously from the late 16th century until it was purchased by the then Pembrokeshire County Council in 1974. It is now one of the museums operated by the Dyfed County Council, but as a fully operational museum it is far from complete.

The Manor House has within it an exhibition relating to the house's past as the home of a notable Pembrokeshire family, and the association of some of its members with the office of Sheriff of Pembrokeshire and the local Hunt. In addition to furnished rooms, the manor also contains a display on the history of photography, while the servants' quarters are being restored to include the furnishings and fittings of an early 19th century kitchen. Only a limited part of Scolton Manor is open to the public, for the building also serves as the administrative headquarters for the staff of the Pembrokeshire Museum Service, and a storage centre for exhibits, documents and books.

The main display area within Scolton Manor Museum is centred on a new exhibition hall, within the walled garden. A display on prehistoric and medieval Pembrokeshire occupies a part of the exhibition hall. The visitor passes through a reconstruction of Hoyle's Mouth Cave, which marks the beginning of a journey through 10,000

Exterior view of Scolton Manor

Three west-Wales coracle types – Teifi, Cleddau and Tywi (l to r)

Saddle-tank locomotive, the 'Margaret'

years of man's progress in south-west Wales. In due course, the museum's collection of farm machinery, industrial and domestic equipment, together with material illustrating the geology and natural history of Pembrokeshire will be shown, but at present much of this material is in store or awaiting restoration. One important collection on display in the exhibition hall relates to the activities of the extensive Llewellin churn works in Haverfordwest. That old-established cooperage, which closed in the 1960s, was the principal supplier of butter churns, cheese vats and other dairying equipment to all of Wales, and also exported worldwide.

The extensive stables at Scolton are devoted to the display of traditional craft equipment used in the old county of Pembrokeshire. South-west Wales was a particularly important centre of rural craftsmanship, for in addition to those craftsmen such as blacksmiths and saddlers who supplied local needs, a number of others came into existence to utilise local raw materials. In the north of the county, for example, the bowl-turning and spoon-carving industry attained national fame due to the plentiful supply of sycamore in the moist river valleys, while the woollen industry flourished in the Preseli foothills, in an area of sheep farming and power-providing mountain streams. Unfortunately, these important local industries are not as yet interpreted at Scolton.

Llewellin's Triangular Churn

Between the stables and exhibition hall a railway exhibition is being prepared. This will illustrate the involved and exciting railway history of Pembrokeshire, and the centrepiece is the 0–6–0 saddle-tank locomotive, 'Margaret', built for the Rosebush Quarries by a British manufacturer in 1878. A number of exhibits from the old Maenclochog and Rosebush Railway Company will be displayed. This unusual railway, which meandered its way through the Preseli foothills, was once the main link between London and the Irish Packet port of Fishguard. Despite the optimism of its directors, who even started creating a corrugated-iron tourist town in the remote village of Rosebush, the railway was doomed to failure once the main Great Western Railway line to Fishguard was opened.

Scolton Manor Museum is in the early stage of development, but bearing in mind the rich cultural heritage of south-west Wales it could become a major regional museum.

KIDWELLY

Kidwelly Industrial Museum

Kidwelly, Dyfed SA17 4LW
(0554) 891078
Open daily Easter to September (closed weekend mornings). £ ☕ P ♿ W
🚻 & 👥 preferably book in advance, especially if guided tour required.

What the slate industry was to Gwynedd, the tinplate industry was to the Swansea region. In 1913 four out of every five tinplate workers in the United Kingdom lived within a twenty-mile radius of Swansea, and the whole economy of towns and villages such as **Llanelli**, Morriston, Briton Ferry and Gorseinon was tied up with the tinplate industry, which gave employment to men, women and children. Llanelli was once known as 'Tinopolis' because there was such a concentration of tin works in the surrounding area.

Tinplate – iron or steel bar rolled into sheets and coated with tin – was first made in Wales in the late 17th century, but it was during the 18th century that the industry really developed in south-west Wales. The rapid growth of the Welsh tinplate industry was due to the development of the United States of America: tinplate provided cheap material for the domestic utensils needed by the pioneering families of the New World, a roofing material for their homesteads, drums for the developing oil industry, and cans for the meat produce of Chicago and fruit farmed in California. So successful was the Welsh tinplate industry that in 1891 President McKinley imposed a tariff on all imported tinplate. West Wales suffered badly; tinplate workers emigrated to the USA by the thousand, and many works in the Swansea Valley closed, never to open again.

This labour intensive, very Welsh industry deserves a full interpretation, but it was not until the opening of the Kidwelly Industrial Museum in 1982 that an attempt was made to provide such a facility. Unfortunately, much of the original equipment associated with the Kidwelly Tinplate Works had been removed for scrap in the 1970s, so that the opportunity of creating a comprehensive and evocative facility was lost forever. Nevertheless, a great deal has been done to redevelop the site, but it is a presentation of relics rather than the preservation of a complete works. Pit-head gear from the nearby Morlais Colliery has been re-erected on the site; there are two locomotives, a steam crane and a number of exhibits relating to the tinplate industry moved to Kidwelly from other works in the region. Among surviving relics that were used on the site itself are the remains of a water-powered mill, a large 'Foden' steam engine (which powered the hot rolls and cropping shears) and a horizontal steam engine.

The Kidwelly Tinplate Works, according to a plaque affixed to an office building at the entrance to the site, was rebuilt in 1801 and was 'the oldest in the kingdom'. The site was occupied originally by a stamping mill, which was taken over by Charles Gwynn, who established a water-powered tinplate works there in 1737.

Aerial view of Kidwelly Industrial Museum

Steam power was introduced in the 1860s, and the works were in continuous use until 1941. Located on the banks of the river Gwendraeth Fach, the thirteen-acre site today consists of four original buildings, which comprise the box room, assorting room, cold rolls, engine house, mess-room, and a chimney stack and machinery.

The main aim of the museum is to reconstruct as much as possible the tinplate process and to interpret it to the visiting public. It sets out to illustrate the methods of producing tinplate while also providing an insight into the desperately hard life of the tinplate worker. In addition the museum aims to record and preserve material relating to the other industries of the **Llanelli** area, which in recent years has suffered greatly from the process of de-industrialisation.

These are early days at Kidwelly: a great deal has been achieved within a few years, and there is no doubt that the museum has the potential to develop into a first-class recreational and educational facility. It is run by Kidwelly Museum Trust in conjunction with Llanelli Borough Council, and is one of the main attractions in the area. At present, interpretation is basic and visitors guide themselves around the site following a route set out in the printed guide. Eventually it is hoped to bring the museum to life by turning the machinery, having 'workers' in costume explaining the process, and encouraging craftsmen to work here.

To the east of Llanelli, in the shadow of the modern *Trostre Tinplate Works*, a small museum has been established at the former Trostre farm. Visits to this can only be made by prior arrangement with the Works Manager. Trostre Farm itself, rethatched and renovated, contains a fascinating exhibition of small items including tinplate workers' dress, and a can of the first beer canned in tinplate for the nearby Felinfoel Brewery. The area around **Llanelli** was famous for its tinplate; hence the saucepans on top of the rugby goalposts at the famous Stradey Park, and the old song '*Sospan Fach*' (Little saucepan), the battle cry of all who owe allegiance to this fascinating Welsh town.

A rollerman entering a 'single' into rolls at a tinplate works

LLANBERIS

Amgueddfa'r Gogledd: Museum of the North

Llanberis, Gwynedd LL55 4UR
(0286) 871331
Open daily. W
& book in advance.

The village of Llanberis, located at the foot of Wales' highest mountain, was in the past concerned overwhelmingly with the production of slate. Dominating the village is the huge Dinorwig Quarry, rising in steps to a height of 1,400 feet above the level of Llyn Peris. That huge quarry, which employed 4,000 men and boys at the height of its activity, was finally closed in 1969 and a village that depended almost entirely on 'the most Welsh of Welsh industries' went through a period of unprecedented depression. Nevertheless, the spectacular scenery of the Llanberis area – its lakes and mountains, and indeed the remains of the slate industry – provided the basis of another activity, that of tourism. The Llanberis of today is a summer honeypot for tourism, and a number of facilities that cater for the visitor's needs have flourished within the village. Here is located the Padarn Country Park with its **Welsh Slate Museum**, craft workshops and lakeside narrow-gauge railway. Here, too, the spectacular Snowdon mountain railway has its terminus, and the unbelievable Pump Storage hydro-electric scheme, opened in 1984 and a monument to the skills of modern engineers, attracts many thousands of visitors, who are able to visit the vast man-made caverns that accommodate turbines and other machinery.

One of the latest attractions of Llanberis is Amgueddfa'r Gogledd – the Museum of the North, which opened as the North Wales branch of the **National Museum of Wales** in the summer of 1989. It is a joint venture between the National Museum and the National Grid Division of the Central Electricity Generating Board, and the

Interior view of the Museum of the North

attraction is presented as 'The Power of Wales'. The most modern and sophisticated technology is used to take the visitor on a fascinating journey through time accompanied by the Welsh wizard, Merlin. He is the ideal host: 'I was here before the sunrise and the first dawn, before the wind blew and the rain fell; I saw the hills rise and the seas form, I noticed the first flower open. There is nothing here that I have not seen, nothing in this land that is not known to me. For I am Merlin, the one who sees; I know the power of the land, the land of Wales'. Merlin conducts the visitor through a series of tableaux with life-sized 'talking heads' that present the turbulent story of the people of Wales. Three-dimensional objects, maps and illustrations are an integral part of the exhibition, which is aimed at those people who may not be aware of 'The Power of Wales'.

The journey through time begins long before the appearance of man, striving to conquer his environment, with the force of volcanoes, ice and water shaping the landscape of Wales. This leads to an environmental display of the rich varieties of plant and animal life, and the development of agriculture and the rural economy. North Wales is renowned for its natural beauty. The plants, animals, rocks and dramatic landforms of the area are featured in the natural sciences theatre, which has been packed with the latest technology in order to create a novel way of presenting familiar sights and sounds.

Visitors are taken along a route that explores the history of Wales, in particular the North. Along the way they meet the people that shaped the face of Wales: the Celts – proud warriors whose secret power was the blacksmith's forge and who built their forts around the ridges of hilltops; the Druids, who used their power in cruel exploitations; the Romans, with power of intellect and discipline, among them Magnus Maximus, the Roman Commander closly associated with *Segontium* (Caernarfon), where according to

Reconstruction, Bronze Age warriors in combat, 1100 BC ('Warriors, Druids & Slaves')

legend he met and married his dream maiden, Helen. Wales' Patron Saint, Dewi Sant (Saint David), who introduced the power of Christianity, offered protection to communities in hard times. The construction of the great dyke from north to south by King Offa of Saxon Mercia established the Welsh border in the 8th century, before the battle-hardened warlike Normans arrived in the 11th century, with a bitter struggle to exert their power over the Welsh – a struggle that was thwarted by the Welsh princes, supported by the propaganda of the court poets praising the bravery of warriors. Llywelyn ap Gruffydd (Llywelyn ein Llyw Olaf), the last of the Welsh princes, was locked in a power struggle with King Edward I of England who, at enormous expense, built gigantic castles that still stand as a witness to a costly and violent conquest. Owain Glyndwr led a Welsh rebellion to no avail, before Henry VIII gave his seal of approval to an United Kingdom. Later people of power who have shaped the face of Wales are represented by Bishop William Morgan, who translated the Bible into Welsh, and David Lloyd George, who translated the radical and nonconformist traditions of Wales into political power.

The Industrial Revolution in Wales is strikingly presented through showing how Welsh coal fuelled the Revolution and Welsh slate roofed it, while the 'iron mad' John Wilkinson produced parts for James Watt's pioneering steam engines at **Bersham** in North Wales. The quest for Welsh gold and other metals, and the development of the woollen industry, are just some

Bronze bucket from Arthog, Gwynedd, 1000 BC

further elements in the story. The presentation also shows how North Wales responded to industrialisation and the effect that it had on its inhabitants while at the same time the area was being discovered by the tourist in what became a Visitor Revolution.

One of the main functions of Amgueddfa'r Gogledd is to provide a broad insight into the character of the people of Wales. It is a starting point for the exploration of the prehistoric sites and castles, slate villages and harbours that are such a feature of the northern provinces of the Principality. The thrilling multi-media technology of the exhibition, organised by the National Grid Division of the Electricity Generating Board, is aimed at gaining an understanding of how the natural power of water is harnessed to provide electricity. Regular tours of the nearby power station, deep in the Elidir mountain, are organised from the museum.

In addition to 'The Power of Wales' display there is an art gallery and temporary exhibition galleries, where the best of Welsh culture, art and history is presented in a series of regularly changing exhibitions. Some are touring exhibitions organised by other galleries, such as 'Dolbadarn Castle', an exhibition of views by 18th and 19th century tourists, including Richard Wilson and J.M.W. Turner, organised by the **National Library of Wales** (July and August 1990). Many of the exhibitions, however, emanate from the other departments and branches of the **National Museum of Wales**; the major exhibition during the 1990 summer season, for example – 'Warriors, Druids and Slaves – Treasures of later prehistoric and Celtic Wales' – will include about 100 artefacts from the archaeological collections of the National Museum that were originally found in North Wales, among them a gang chain of the early 1st century AD, found at Llyn Cerrig Bach, Anglesey, during the construction of an air force base in 1942. For the first time in its history, the national institution is living up to its name by creating a focus for its activities in the north, well away from the capital city of Cardiff.

1 Right Roman *mould-blown glass bowl, 1st century AD, found at Usk. The Roman Legionary Museum, Caerleon.*

2 Below St Ishmaels *by Graham Sutherland, 1974–75 (inspired by Picton and St Ishmaels, Pembrokeshire). Graham Sutherland Gallery, Haverfordwest.*

3 Above Reconstruction of the environment across southern Wales in late Triassic times, approx. 210 million years ago, when small dinosaurs like this Coelophysis *left footprints in the sand. National Museum of Wales, Cardiff (Dept of Geology).*

4 Left Swansea earthenware jug, painted by Thomas Pardoe, c. 1800. National Museum of Wales, Cardiff (Dept of Art).

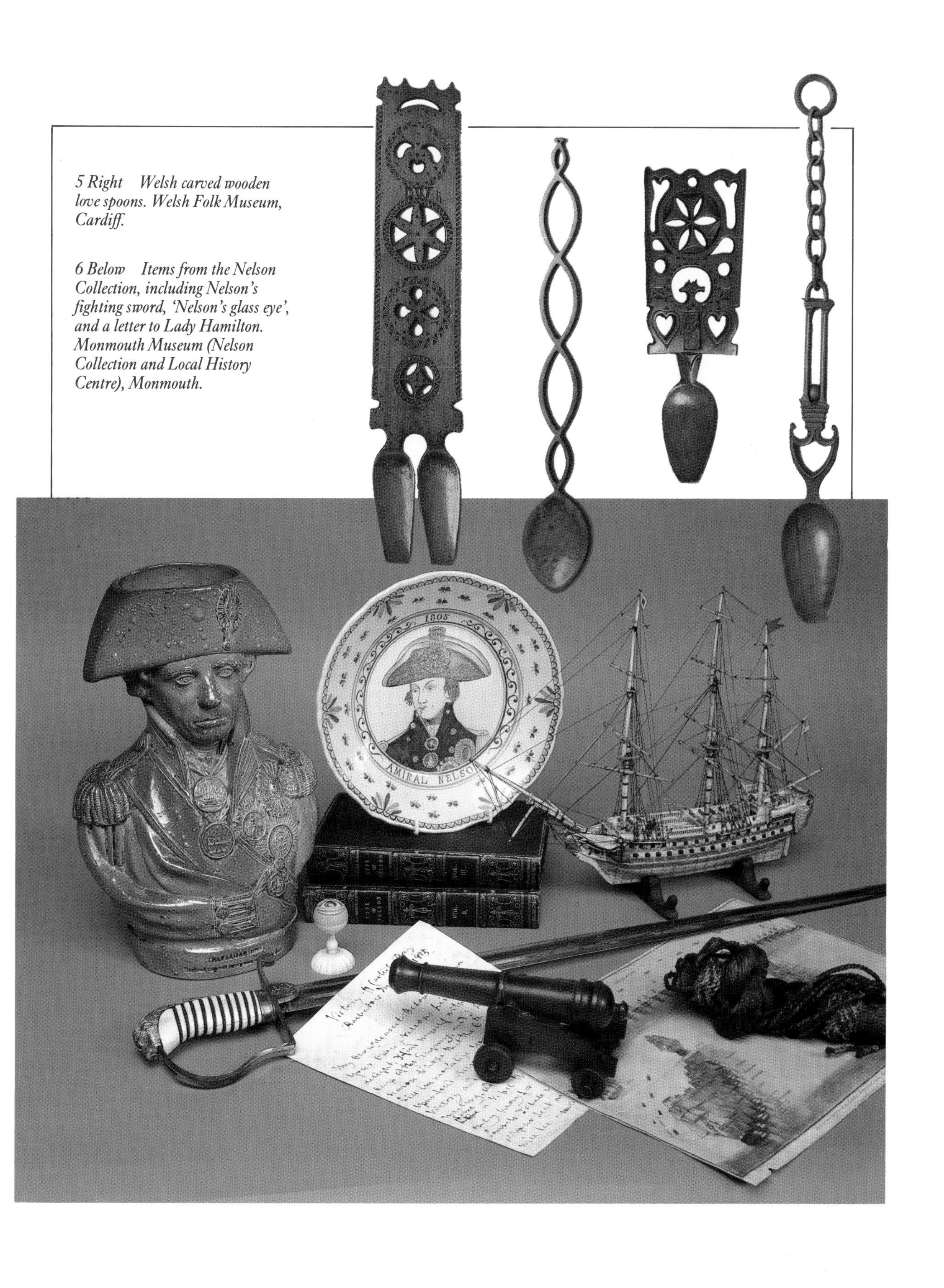

5 Right Welsh carved wooden love spoons. Welsh Folk Museum, Cardiff.

6 Below Items from the Nelson Collection, including Nelson's fighting sword, 'Nelson's glass eye', and a letter to Lady Hamilton. Monmouth Museum (Nelson Collection and Local History Centre), Monmouth.

7 The Tutor *by Augustus John (1878–1961). Glynn Vivian Art Gallery & Museum, Swansea (Gift of Richard J. Strick).*

8 Opposite Floreat *by Cedric Morris (1889–1982). Cyfarthfa Castle Museum, Merthyr Tudful.*

10 Below   Ruby lustre tile made at J.C. Edwards factory, Trefynant, c. 1890. Wrexham Maelor Heritage Centre, Wrexham.

11 Below   Interior view of Penrhos Cottage, Clunderwen.

9 Above   Detail of the National Colour of the 4th Regt, US Infantry, surrendered to the 41st Foot, The Welch Regiment, at Fort Detroit, 1812. The Welch Regiment Museum, Cardiff.

12 Opposite   The Sculpture Gallery, with sculptures of Cupid and Hebe by John Gibson, whose portrait by Margaret Carpenter hangs above the fireplace. Bodelwyddan Castle, Bodelwyddan.

13 The Herb Garden at St Fagans. Welsh Folk Museum, Cardiff.

The Welsh Slate Museum

Gilfach Ddu, Llanberis, Gwynedd LL55 4TY (0286) 870630
Open daily. W
& book in advance, pre-booked parties .

The Welsh slate industry has been described as 'the most Welsh of Welsh Industries', and in 1898, a year that marked the peak of production, no fewer than 15,000 men and boys were employed in the Gwynedd quarrying industry. The products of the slate quarries were exported from specially-constructed ports such as **Porthmadog**, Porth Penrhyn and Port Dinorwic to all parts of the world. The slate quarrying industry gave certain towns and villages, such as Penygroes, Bethesda and *Blaenau Ffestiniog*, their own particular character and personality, and the industry dominated the landscape and the life of Snowdonia.

Located at the foot of Snowdon is the village of Llanberis, today a centre of tourism but once the most important of slate quarrying centres. Dominating the village is the vast Dinorwic Quarry, covering 700 acres of mountainside and rising in steps to a height of 1,400 feet above the lake of Llyn Peris. The quarry, which dates from the late 18th century, became the largest slate quarry in the world, and employed more than 4,000 men and boys. Those quarrymen worked in a harsh and brutalising environment, but nevertheless contributed much to the cultural and literary heritage of Wales. Towards the end of 1969 the Dinorwic Quarry closed, but the central workshops below the quarry on the banks of the lake (Llyn Padarn) were acquired by the then Caernarvonshire County Council for guardianship by the Department of the Environment. The **National Museum of Wales** was invited to set up a museum relating to the slate industry within the so-called Gilfach Ddu workshops. While the fabric of the building is the responsibility of CADW, who succeeded the Department of the Environment and the Welsh Office as guardians, the organisation of the exhibition and the care of the machinery and contents of the building are all the responsibility of the National Museum of Wales. Its role here is the preservation, study and interpretation of material that relates to the history of the Welsh slate industry in all parts of the Principality.

Exterior view of the Dinorwic Quarry workshops

Located in the centre of the Padarn Country Park, the extensive buildings that now house the museum were erected in 1870, and are reminiscent of a fort in the mountains of Northern India; indeed, the association of the masters of the Dinorwic Quarry in the late 19th century with the outposts of the British Empire may explain the fortlike appearance of the workshops. During the working life of the quarry, the needs for new machinery and plant, as well as the continuing maintenance of equipment, railway rolling stock, and even the steamships that carried slate from Y Felinheli, renamed Port Dinorwic, were all met by the highly skilled craftsmen of Gilfach Ddu. It had an iron casting workshop and a brass foundry; it had its contingent of highly skilled pattern-makers and metal founders; and it had locomotive

Slate splitting

engineers, blacksmiths and other skilled men, so that the Dinorwic Quarry was a self-sufficient unit, its workshops capable of meeting all the needs of an important industrial undertaking. Most of the machinery once used to maintain the equipment of quarrying is still in place at the museum, and much of it is in full working order. Visitors are shown the techniques of blacksmithing, iron and brass founding, as well as splitting and trimming slates by the museum staff, all of whom once worked in the slate quarries. Thus, the Welsh Slate Museum is a living museum staffed by Welsh-speaking craftsmen who have spent a lifetime in the slate industry; the integrity and authenticity of the institution are above reproach.

Power for the machines was provided by a huge cast-iron water-wheel, said to be the largest in Wales, which draws its power from a water pipe that runs for miles from the northern slope of Snowdon. This impressive structure has been fully restored by the museum's craftsmen, for the self-sufficiency of the complex is still an important element in its development.

In addition to the preservation of important items of machinery in an authentic setting, the museum also sets out to interpret the economic, social and cultural history of the slate-quarrying communities. The interpretative exhibition in the north wing of the complex accommodates an audio-visual theatre, and an exhibition area that emphasises the character of Welsh slate-quarrying communities. Either by organised Land-Rover excursions or by following the zig-zag paths once trodden by quarrymen, visitors are able to gain access to the vast complex of galleries on the mountainside above Llyn Padarn and Llyn Peris. Here may be seen the railed inclines that rise steeply from gallery to gallery, and the canteens and blast shelters that were an integral part of every slate quarry. Here and there, too, are the barracks that once accommodated the itinerant workers who came from all parts of North Wales to follow one of the most dangerous of all extractive industries.

The transportation of slate from quarry to seaport was a vital element in the industry and the Gwynedd quarries depended very heavily on a network of narrow-gauge railways that were designed specifically for traversing difficult country. The Padarn Lake Railway, with its terminus near the Welsh Slate Museum, runs a regular train service along the north shore of the lake, and occasionally the museum operates some of the rail wagons it has collected from a large number of quarries along the line of the Lake Railway. 'The Slate Museum Special' is drawn by the museum's own maroon-coloured steam locomotive, 'Una'. Unfortunately the railway track no longer extends as far as the purpose-built Port Dinorwic on the shores of the Menai Straits.

At the Welsh Slate Museum, and at the other attractions within the Padarn Country Park including the **Museum of the North**, both an industry and a unique culture are interpreted. 'In the quarries themselves', wrote one observer in 1933, 'English is a foreign tongue and those shapeless monotonous villages which flank them; grey and drab but clean . . . are the homes of a vigorous native culture'. That culture is what is being presented at Amgueddfa Lechi Cymru (the Welsh Slate Museum).

LLANDRINDOD WELLS

Llandrindod Wells Museum

Temple Street, Llandrindod Wells, Powys LD1 5DL (0597) 4513
Closed lunchtimes, Saturday afternoons and all day Sundays. F
♿ S: wheelchair access difficult.
🚻 & 👥 book in advance.

Llandrindod Wells Museum, pleasantly situated in a small park in the centre of the most important of Welsh spa towns, was established in 1932, specifically to display an excavated dug-out canoe that had been found locally in 1929. Although its golden era as one of the most important of Welsh resorts has long passed, the town's huge hotels and boating lake, theatre and numerous places of worship remind the visitor that Llandrindod Wells was the boom town of late Victorian and Edwardian Wales, when summer visitors came in droves, principally to take the medicinal waters.

The ground floor exhibition area in the museum is devoted to the history of Llandrindod as a spa town, and here the visitor is able to obtain a picture of the social life, the pastimes and the business of the town's inhabitants and

Part of the laundry display

General View from Golf Links.

ANGLING in preserved waters.

GOLF on perfect courses.

BOATING on the famous Lake.

BOWLS on first-class greens.

TENNIS Hard and grass courts.

PUTTING on the best of courses.

SWIMMING in new open-air pool.

WALKS through ideal country.

Shakey Bridge on River Ithon.

" Your Spa is in a lovely setting! "
—H.R.H. The Prince of Wales

UNSURPASSED NATURAL

Sulphur and Saline Waters

The waters are classified in three groups—the Saline waters, the Sulphur waters, and the Chalybeate waters.

Among the waters from the Saline group, one contains a definite amount of Lithia, while two others are very rich in Calcium.

The Sulphur water gives evidence of quite definite radio activity, and the gaseous content of this water is very high.

The Saline waters are laxative and aperient in sufficient doses. The Sulphur waters are diuretic, and of course the Chalybeate water is an excellent tonic.

Sulphur Baths and Treatments.

The **Bathing Establishments** are thoroughly equipped with all modern apparatus, and the treatments are carefully carried out.

The electrical department is exceedingly complete.

Good Health means Happiness

Pen-y-Garreg Dam in Elan Valley.

TOUR WALES BY CAR.

Make one of the Llandrindod Wells Hotels your Headquarters and do the loop Tours to North, South, East and West, returning each day.

GARAGE ACCOMMODATION.

Visitors coming to Llandrindod Wells by Car will find ample facilities for garaging. **The Automobile Palace** is recommended. (Managing Director, Tom Norton).

The 18th Hole at Woodlands Putting Course.

LLANDRINDOD WELLS THE FAMOUS WELSH SPA.

Poster advertising the attractions of Llandrindod Wells

visitors. The story of Llandrindod Wells is an exciting one, for although the medicinal qualities of the wells were realised in the late 17th century it was not until the arrival of the Central Wales Railway, which ran from Swansea to Shrewsbury, that development in Llandrindod took off to meet the needs of Victorian visitors. Between 1865 and 1914 the appearance of Llandrindod was that of a boom town. Hotels and boarding houses sprang up along the new streets, and new shops were opened to meet the needs of visitors and residents. Many of the private houses were built on a grand scale. The 'season' lasted from May to mid-September, and outside the pump room visitors queued each morning, entertained by music from the resident orchestras. There were baths providing a wide range of modern treatments, and all kinds of pastimes, from horse racing to tennis, concerts to plays, were catered for. Llandrindod Wells was really the mecca of Edwardian Wales; it had all the essentials of a thriving seaside resort, without the sea.

Although the interpretation of a spa town forms the core of the display at the Llandrindod Wells Museum, other aspects of local history are not neglected. Man's early activities in the area are represented by finds and discoveries made at the fort of Castell Collen near the town. Castell Collen was excavated between 1911–14, and between 1954–57. Pottery, metalwork and items of jewellery found are on exhibition.

An interesting collection, although perhaps of little local significance, is the Paterson collection of 'Dolls in National Costume'. These were brought back by a member of the Old Radnorshire museum committee during the trips he made to many parts of the world. Another interesting collection is that of samplers dating from 1749 to 1865, completed by girls in successive generations of a local family.

LLANDUDNO

Llandudno Museum (The Chardon Trust)

Chardon House,
17–19 Gloddaeth Street,
Llandudno, Gwynedd LL30 2DD
(0492) 76517

Scheduled to open summer 1990; check with museum. W
& prior notice preferred.

Llandudno's new museum, scheduled to open in summer 1990, will interpret the history of this most flourishing and desirable of North Wales seaside resorts. Its emphasis on local history and archaeology, and its thematic displays, will be in complete contrast to the old Rapallo House Museum, whose holdings form the core of the new Llandudno Museum's collections.

Rapallo House Museum was above all an art gallery and a memorial to its benefactor. Until 1985, it was situated in Rapallo House, an amazing mock-Tudor period piece on the eastern outskirts of Llandudno that had been lived in for several years by Francis Edouard Chardon (1865–1925), a wealthy amateur artist and collector, who on his death bequeathed the house and its contents in trust as a museum and art gallery for the benefit of Llandudno's inhabitants and visitors. Chardon was the son of an indigo planter of French extraction who owned considerable property in Bengal; his mother, Maria Theresa née Rapallo, was the daughter of a rich industrialist and shipowner. Like many wealthy young men, he studied art abroad, and took up watercolour painting and pastel drawing. The somewhat mediocre collection that he left included many of his own works as well as paintings, drawings, sculptures, and miniatures by other artists. Rapallo House Museum also had a reconstructed 'Welsh kitchen', apparently incorporating the contents of a cottage at Llanberis in the heart of Snowdonia that Chardon had bought during the few years that he spent in North Wales, but 'no attempt' had been made 'to reconstruct in detail any known example of an old-fashioned Welsh kitchen', as Isaac Williams (a former Keeper at the National Museum of Wales) noted in his guidebook to the museum of 1926.

With a collection of limited interest, Rapallo House Museum was a period piece that attracted few visitors and no educational parties. The new Llandudno Museum promises to be modern and exciting, but it will no longer have a close association with Francis Edouard Chardon – bachelor, painter, eccentric and man of private means. The only visible remnant of the old Rapallo House Museum will be the reconstructed Welsh kitchen, which apparently had been the most popular part of that museum.

The emphasis of the new museum will shift from art to local history and archaeology. The first phase to open will trace the story of the Llandudno area up to the point where the surveyor, Owen Williams, conceived his vision of the perfectly-planned Victorian seaside resort in the mid-19th century. Displays will begin with the prehistoric collections, shown in a 'cave' (the presence of which, in great numbers, was the reason that early man settled here). The Llandudno area is rich in archaeological material and recent discoveries on Great Orme, the hilly peninsula that overlooks the tranquil bay, indicate that it may have been the site of some of the earliest copper mining in Europe, dating back to the Bronze Age. The area is also rich in Roman remains, and material

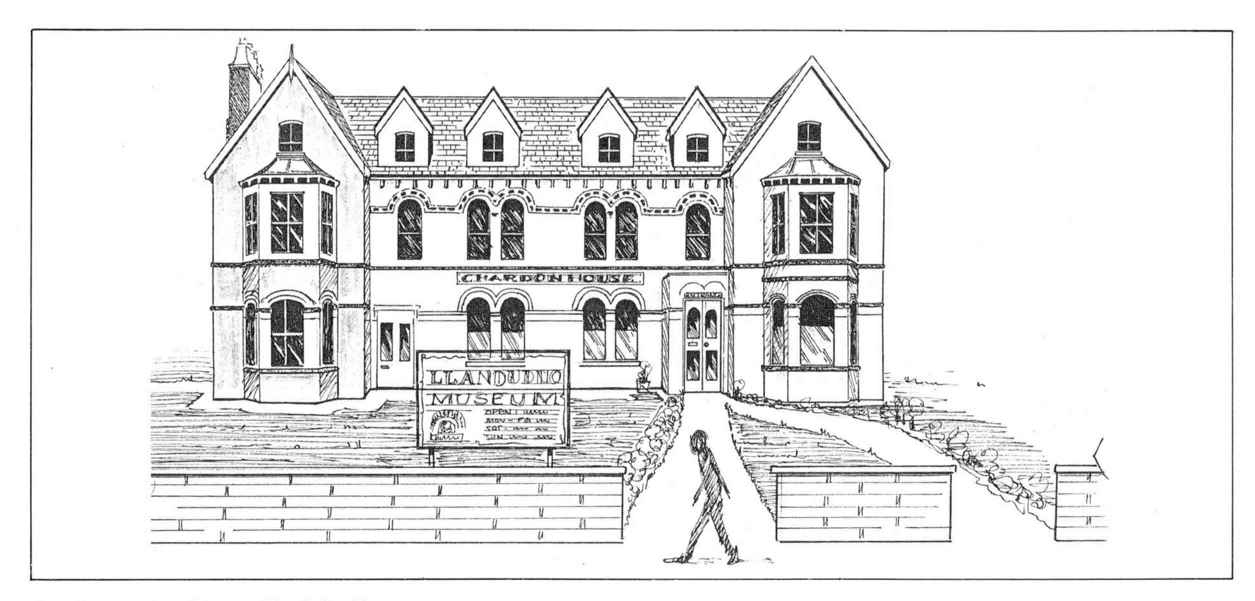

Artist's impression of the new Llandudno Museum

excavated from the Conwy Valley fort of *Kanovium* at Caerhun, seven miles from Llandudno, will form the nucleus of the Roman display. The Dark Ages and the medieval period will also be interpreted. This part of North Wales was, after all, the region of impressive castles, with Deganwy Castle (an important focus of Welsh resistance to the English, as well as allegedly being the home of the 6th century king, Maelgwyn) and the stupendous Conwy Castle, build by Edward I opposite Deganwy, in close proximity to the town. Later exhibits will be related primarily to copper mining; mining was the main source of the town's livelihood until Llandudno's 19th century 'conversion' into a seaside resort.

The second phase of the displays, which the museum hopes to complete in the next year or so, will continue the story of Llandudno and its development as an important holiday resort.

The new museum will accommodate a temporary exhibition gallery: the first exhibition will be on the theme of Llandudno during the Second World War, prepared by the Llandudno Historical Society. An active programme of events and activities has already begun with local schools. Children will be specially catered for – in direct contrast to Chardon's own wishes, for his will stipulated that no one under sixteen years of age should be allowed into his museum. The Chardon spirit has finally been exorcised!

Llandudno still has a gallery devoted to art – the Mostyn Gallery, opened in 1979. It takes its name from the gallery that was built in 1898 by Lady Augusta Mostyn to show paintings from the Mostyn collection, which ceased to function at the outbreak of the First World War. The new gallery occupies purpose-built premises in Vaughan Street, Llandudno, and is administered by a limited company receiving funds from the Welsh Arts Council, North Wales Arts Association, Aberconwy District Council and Gwynedd County Council. Its primary purpose is to stage temporary art exhibitions from a variety of sources and it could certainly develop into one of the principal art galleries in Wales.

LLANELLI

Parc Howard Museum and Art Gallery

Llanelli, Dyfed SA15 3AS
(0554) 773538
Closed Sunday mornings April to October, and weekends November to March. F
♿ S: wheelchair access difficult.
🚻 & 👫 welcome.

Llanelli, a town of some 40,000 inhabitants (but the borough town of a district with 74,000 residents), is located at the western extremity of industrial South Wales. Famous for its tinplate industry, beer brewing and rugby, it has suffered very greatly in recent years from an industrial malaise that has seen the closure of most of its major industrial undertakings and an unacceptably high level of unemployment amongst its inhabitants. As with so many other authorities witnessing the decimation of its industrial base, the Llanelli Borough Council has turned towards leisure and tourism as a possible elixir that could solve its problems. The Pembrey Peninsula is being developed as a country park and leisure centre; **Kidwelly**, with its historical castle, now has an industrial museum; and tourists are being encouraged to visit the 'saucepan town': 'There is a bit more to Llanelli than you may have thought', says the local tourist guide, 'so next time you're planning a holiday or even a short break, why not visit Llanelli; you'll be pleasantly surprised'.

One of the minor attractions of Llanelli is the local art gallery, situated in parkland about a quarter of a mile from the town centre at Parc Howard. The Parc Howard Museum and Art Gallery, in the care of the Borough's public librarian, is located in a Victorian mansion, known originally as Bryncaerau Castle. This was occupied by the Revd. James Buckley, a prominent early 19th century Methodist minister, and a member of the brewing family whose famous brew has quenched the thirst of many generations of west-Wales industrial workers and rugby followers. In 1885 the mansion was remodelled by the Swansea architect, J.B. Wilson, for J.F.H. Buckley, who sold it in 1912 to Sir Stafford Howard, the Chartered Mayor of

Exterior view of the Parc Howard Museum and Art Gallery

Some of the museum's pieces of Llanelli pottery

Llanelli Borough. Howard bequeathed the house and adjoining parkland to the people of Llanelli as a public park and place of recreation. In 1915 the whole estate was purchased by the Borough Council.

At Parc Howard, four rooms are devoted to a permanent display of Llanelli Borough's collection of paintings; one of these rooms is the Stepney Memorial Gallery, opened in 1962 by Mark Stepney Murray Thriepland 'to commemorate the jubilee of the gift of this park to the people of Llanelli'. An upstairs room is devoted to the work of local artists such as J.D. Innes, a friend of Augustus John, and the excellent Evan Walters of Swansea.

The other room on the first floor contains the finest collection of Llanelli pottery in existence, ranging in date from 1840 to 1921 – the entire period of production of this well-known local pottery. The recent acquisition by the Borough of Mr Robert Pugh's collection of several thousand items greatly enhanced existing holdings. The Llanelli Pottery was started by William Chambers in 1840, and the display includes a small selection of potters' tools and related artefacts. The museum also houses the largest single collection of Welsh ginger beer bottles in existence, consisting of over 16,000 items. Other exhibits depict some aspects of the social and industrial life of Llanelli, and many items are of the nature of personalia relating to local worthies and events – a silver cradle, for example, a set of silver plates, and a souvenir programme of Queen Victoria's visit to Llanelli.

Parc Howard is by modern standards a modest effort; it is currently under financed, as resources have been directed towards the industrial museum at **Kidwelly**, and although a museum officer is employed by the local authority most of her time is likewise devoted to the establishment of that museum. Llanelli, with its wealth of industrial and sporting achievements, deserves better, and the Borough Council is looking for a more centrally sited venue to develop a municipal museum.

The *Llanelli Public Library* in the town centre has an exhibition area with an annual programme of exhibitions by local artists and organisations, and the occasional loan exhibition from various sources. In addition, the Borough Council's contemporary painting collection is housed in the Library and is exhibited regularly. A picture loan scheme is also in operation.

LLANGEFNI

Anglesey Heritage Gallery

Oriel Etifeddiaeth Môn, Llangefni, Gwynedd (0248) 724444
Scheduled to open 1991.

The Island of Anglesey – *Môn Mam Cymru* (Anglesey the Mother of Wales) – has a unique and powerful character that is worthy of interpretation to a wide audience. The geographical, political, historical and linguistic forces that moulded the island have left a legacy of important, tangible remains, and a tradition of cultural development that continues to thrive. The heritage and the uniqueness of Anglesey is crying out for a full-scale museum service to present that rich inheritance, but it was not until October 1987 that the Anglesey Borough Council resolved to 'proceed with the creation of a purpose built gallery in the centre of Llangefni to provide a permanent home for the Tunnicliffe Art Collection. It was resolved that the Gallery would also house the works of other Welsh artists and craftspeople as well as providing a continual programme of temporary exhibitions of an artistic, cultural and heritage nature.' The Heritage Gallery is scheduled to be built at a cost of £1.5 million, with a proposed opening date in 1991. At last 'the Mother of Wales' is to have an institution that its cultural heritage deserves, although the new gallery will be limited at first in its approach to a consideration of arts and artists on the island. Certainly, the archaeology, craft, and industrial, agricultural and maritime history of this unique region of Wales deserves also to be given detailed interpretation.

The impetus for the development of the Heritage Gallery has been the acquisition of the works of Charles Tunnicliffe in 1981 by the Anglesey Borough Council. Charles Tunnicliffe spent most of his working life on the Isle of Anglesey, where he found the inspiration that he needed for his art. The importance of Tunnicliffe's work was assessed by Sir Peter Scott in 1985: 'the verdict of posterity in time to come is likely I believe to rate Charles Tunnicliffe the greatest wildlife artist of the 20th century.' The collection presented to the Anglesey Borough Council comprises an enormous body of reference material, including over 350 measured bird drawings and over fifty working sketchbooks, in addition to a wealth of material, from book illustrations, commissions, and early work, to etchings and engravings. It is a very important collection indeed, and only a very small proportion of the work has ever been seen by the public.

As well as presenting the Tunnicliffe

Charles Tunnicliffe, Study of Lesser black-backed gulls

collection within the context of Anglesey, the gallery will also house the work of other Welsh artists and craftspeople, and stage a programme of temporary exhibitions. The aim of the gallery is to provide a focus for the cultural and artistic activities of Anglesey, to create an asset for the enjoyment and education of islanders and visitors from other areas. It will be a place where local artists can display and see their work, for Anglesey is now the home of a number of eminent artists and a variety of highly-skilled craft workers. The project is indeed a most exciting one.

Charles Tunnicliffe, Studies of Bramblings

LLANGOLLEN

Canal Museum

The Wharf, Llangollen, Clwyd
LL20 8TA (0978) 860702
Open Easter weekend, and daily Whitsun to September.
♿ S: ground floor of museum awkward for wheelchairs, steps to first floor; good access to horse-drawn boats.
& book in advance if 30 or more; 25% deposit and one month's notice required.

The Canal Museum and Exhibition Centre, on a wharf in the beautiful town of Llangollen, was established in 1974 to interpret the story of the canals of Britain with the help of working and static models and audio-visual material. The Llangollen Canal, with its fleet of operating boats, is an integral part of the establishment, and a number of trips on horse-drawn passenger boats are on offer to the visiting public. The Vale of Llangollen is scenically very beautiful, and passenger services have operated along the canal since 1884, when Llangollen was coming into its own as a holiday resort of importance.

The Canal Museum, however, does not limit its interest to the Llangollen Canal alone, for it sets out to trace the history of canals, though not in any detail, throughout the United Kingdom. It contains a reconstruction of a 19th century coal mine, and points to the importance of canals in the transportation of that raw material. The economic importance of canals in developing the industrial regions of Britain is described, and exhibits and photographs show what types of cargo were carried and how these cargoes were handled. The civil engineering problems of canal construction are carefully interpreted. Also illustrated is the way of life of the people who built and worked on Britain's first major transport system, and the wildlife to be found along the canals. The exhibition

The Pontcysyllte Aqueduct, carrying the Llangollen Canal over the river Dee

centre is housed in an early 19th century warehouse on the canal wharf, and through films, slides, and working and static models, the story of canals in Britain unfolds in an entertaining way.

Of course, a visit to the Canal Museum is incomplete without a boat trip along the Llangollen Canal. Regular excursions run from the museum. Along the towpath, sheltered by overhanging trees, horses gently pull passenger-carrying canal boats along one of the most spectacular stretches of inland waterway in Britain. The Llangollen Canal, which enters Wales at Chirk, is a section of the Shropshire Union Canal system engineered by Telford and Jessop. It was originally intended to link the border towns of Shrewsbury and Chester via the ironworks at Wrexham, and the brick and tile manufacturing centres at Ruabon.

One of the most spectacular feats of engineering that can be visited from the Canal Museum is the Pontcysyllte Aqueduct, 4½ miles east of Llangollen. Thomas Telford built this masterpiece of engineering to carry the canal at a height of 127 feet above the river Dee. Nineteen sets of arches, each with a span of 53 feet making a total length of 1007 feet, carry the cast-iron trough of the canal and towpath.

In the Canal Museum itself, which is really the centre for excursions, there is a shop selling books and pictures, as well as a wide selection of traditionally-painted canal ware. There are water cans, jugs, bowls and mugs, many of them carrying the traditional rose-and-castle decoration in bright colours usually associated with the people that worked the canals of Britain.

The Canal Museum and Wharf, where canal boat trips begin

ECTARC – European Centre for Traditional and Regional Cultures

Parade Street, Llangollen, Clwyd LL20 8RB (0978) 861514
Closed all day Sunday October to Easter, and otherwise on Sunday mornings. F P ♿ W
& preferably book in advance: contact Education Officer.

The town of Llangollen, once renowned for woollen manufacturing and coracle fishing, occupies a beautiful site on the banks of the river Dee. Since 1945 it has gained international associations in that it is the venue of the International Eisteddfod where for a week in July every year, singers and dancers in colourful national costume bring life to what is really quite a small country town. Those international connections of Llangollen are not limited to a single week at the height of summer, for in 1983 an important international institution was established in the town, known originally as the European Centre for Folk Studies. The centre occupied premises in a Victorian school building in one of Llangollen's side streets. In 1988, however, the institution changed its name to the European Centre for Traditional and Regional Cultures, and the old Baptist Chapel, a landmark in one of the main streets of Llangollen, was acquired to provide additional facilities. Although the original character of the chapel as a typical nonconformist place of worship has been preserved, the interior has been converted to provide a first-class modern auditorium and an extensive exhibition hall. ECTARC seeks to promote the traditional and regional cultures of Europe through performances, exhibitions and research. Countries and regions are invited to provide exhibitions relating to their own cultures, usually for a period of up to two years. This exciting new venture will serve to bring the rich heritage of traditional cultures in Europe to a much wider public. In addition, various exhibitions from Wales have been organised for showing in centres on the continent.

Exterior view of the European Centre for Traditional and Regional Cultures

Display of Romanian folk dress

The town of Llangollen has also a number of other attractions. Vale Crucis Abbey, founded in 1201 by the Cistercian monks, is large and impressive, while the mansion of Plas Newydd, a beautiful black and white house that served as a home for the renowned if eccentric 'Ladies of Llangollen', is a considerable attraction. The *Railway Museum* at Llangollen Station, with locomotives and rolling stock, is the centre for steam-hauled passenger trains, while a more relaxed mode of transport is provided by the horse-drawn canal boats that run along the beautiful Vale of Llangollen.

LLANIDLOES

Museum of Local History & Industry

Old Market Hall, Llanidloes, Powys SY18 6AD
(enquiries to *Powysland Museum, Salop Road, Welshpool SY21 7EG (0938) 4759*)
Open Easter week, and daily (except lunchtimes) from Spring Bank Holiday to end of September. F
♿ S: no wheelchair access to museum.
🚻 & 👥 book in advance if talk requried.

Chartist relics

This museum occupies the only black and white market hall that survives in Wales. The timber-framed building, with one end of stone and the other of brick, stands on the cross-roads in the middle of the small mid-Wales market town of Llanidloes. Underneath the black and white structure is an open market place with cobbled paving. Above it, supported an oak beams and arches, is an old court room that now houses the Museum of Local History and Industry (administered by the **Powysland Museum**). From the roof rises a cupola in which hangs the market bell.

Llanidloes is an ancient town. It was granted a charter in 1280 whereby two annual fairs and a weekly market on Saturdays were allowed. In addition to being an important market town for an

The Market Hall, Llanidloes, from an old photograph

The old Market Hall building today

extensive agricultural hinterland throughout the centuries, it was also an important centre of industry, and that industrial activity is represented in the contents of this small museum.

It has, inevitably, a reconstructed Welsh kitchen, but also a number of relics connected with the Chartist outbreak of 1839. A town that was the centre of flannel manufacturing was understandably in the forefront of the Chartist movement, and 1839 was a year of unprecedented violence amongst the textile workers of Llanidloes. The woollen factories of Llanidloes flourished tremendously in the early 19th century, and a large proportion of the population of the town, both male and female, was connected with the manufacture of flannel. A government report of 1838 states that as many as 795 of the inhabitants of the town were hand-loom weavers, either working in their homes or in factory buildings: a group of workers who, according to the then vicar of Llanidloes, were noted for 'insubordination, the defiance of all authority, drunkenness, dishonesty and fighting'. Llanidloes in the 1830s was indeed an exciting town, but unfortunately that excitement is not conveyed to the museum visitor.

The museum also has a small archaeological collection of fragments excavated from the Roman fort at nearby Caersws, and the usual collection of domestic utensils used by the farming families of the district.

LLANYSTUMDWY

The Lloyd George Museum

Llanystumdwy, Cricieth, Gwynedd
(0766) 522071
(enquiries to *Gwynedd Archives and Museums Service, County Offices, Caernarfon, Gwynedd LL55 1SH*)
Open daily Easter, and May to September, otherwise by appointment. £
♿ S: wheelchair access difficult.
book in advance with museum, or Museums Officer (0286) 4121 ext. 2098.
book in advance with Education Officers, Gwynedd Archives (0286) 4121 ext. 2090/2091.

It was Winston Churchill who said, 'As a man of action, resource and creative energy, he stood, when on his zenith, without a rival. He was the greatest Welshman that the unconquerable race has produced since the age of the Tudors. Much of his work abides, some of it will grow greatly in the future and those who come after us will find the pillars of his life's toil upstanding, massive and indestructible. The greater part of our fortunes in peace and war were shaped by this one man.'

The small museum located two miles west of Cricieth is devoted to the memory of a man who was probably one of the greatest statesmen Wales ever produced. Born to Welsh parents in Manchester in 1863, David Lloyd George came to the small village of Llanystumdwy to be brought up by his cobbler uncle after the death of his father in 1864. It was in a small cottage, 'Highgate', now a part of the

Highgate, Lloyd George's boyhood home, Llanystumdwy

Portrait of David Lloyd George

A Freedom Casket

Lloyd George Museum, that he spent his childhood. In 1890 he became member of parliament for the Caernarfon Boroughs, and as Chancellor of the Exchequer, Minister of Munitions, and Prime Minister, he became one of the most powerful men in the world. Despite his fame, he never lost touch with the village of Llanystumdwy, and it was here that he died as the first Earl Dwyfor in 1945. He was buried on the banks of the River Dwyfor, and from his grave runs a path to the small museum dedicated to him. This museum is now in the process of being enlarged and developed. It will include an extensive exhibition tracing the career of Lloyd George, an audio-visual theatre, and a bookshop. A study centre concerned in particular with material representing Lloyd George's period and interests will be set up.

In addition to the memorial museum and the grave designed by Lloyd George's great friend, the notable architect, Clough Williams Ellis, the village of Llanystumdwy has many other buildings associated with the statesman. A self-conducted village walk has been prepared as an integral element in the presentation. Highgate, his boyhood home, and Tŷ Newydd, Lloyd George's last home, may be seen, as can the village school where he was educated and the beautiful Moriah Chapel where he worshipped. After winning a libel action in 1909, Lloyd George helped finance a village institute, which is also incorporated into the village walk. During his boyhood Lloyd George spent much of his time in the village smithy with the blacksmith Hugh Jones. In a speech in 1909, he said 'Yonder smithy was my first Parliament, where night after night we discussed and decided all the obtruse questions relating to this world and the next, in politics, theology, in philosophy and science. There was nothing too wide and comprehensive for us to discuss and we settled all the problems among ourselves without the slightest misgiving'. Undoubtedly, the small village of Llanystumdwy was an immense influence in the life of the great statesman, and the museum, when it is fully developed, will serve as a worthy memorial to this most distinguished of Welshmen.

For younger visitors to Llanystumdwy, a Nature Trail has been prepared that begins in St John's churchyard and carries on to Lloyd George's grave and along the river Dwyfor.

MERTHYR TUDFUL

Cyfarthfa Castle Museum

Cyfarthfa Castle, Cyfarthfa Park, Merthyr Tudful, Mid Glamorgan CF47 8RE (0685) 723112
Closed lunchtimes and Sunday mornings.
S: wheelchair access difficult.
& book in advance; schoolroom available.

Cyfarthfa Castle from the lake

The town of Merthyr Tudful in the 19th century was a boom town that drew people from all parts of the country to work in its numerous coal mines and ironworks. Ironstone occurred naturally in the area, and there were ample woodlands to be converted into charcoal for firing furnaces; as the forests were denuded, the area was fortunate in having rich seams of coking coal. Merthyr, a rough, tough town, grew with great rapidity to become the largest and most industrialised of all the settlements of South Wales. It attracted the English ironmasters – the Guests, Bacons, Crawshays, Homfreys and Hills – to seek their fortunes in the hills, turning the towns and villages of the region into world leaders in iron production and the mining of coal.

One of the best known of the dynasties of iron-masters who came to Merthyr Tudful was the Crawshay family, who in 1765 established the vast Cyfarthfa ironworks, which supplied pig iron to the world. In 1825, William Crawshay had the noble and splendid Cyfarthfa Castle built as his family home. Surrounded by 160 acres of parkland, and built by Robert Lugar in the Gothick style, the house overlooked the spreading mass of the Cyfarthfa ironworks, which had brought great wealth to its owner. The grandest ironmaster's house in South Wales provided the setting for the lavish entertainment of famous personalities from Victorian society. 'Mr. Crawshay's ironworks at Cyfarthfa', said one early-19th century observer, 'are by far the largest in Europe and in that case, as far as we know, the largest in the world. He employs constantly fifteen hundred men at an average of thirty shillings a week per man'. During the last quarter of the 19th century there was a gradual decline in iron production in Merthyr as the industry moved to the seaboard of Glamorgan. Cyfarthfa Castle remained the family home of the rich Crawshay dynasty until the 1880s and then fell into neglect; in 1909 the newly-formed Merthyr Tudful Borough Council bought the castle. The luxurious apartments, the scene of so many splendid occasions in previous years, were converted into a museum, while another part became the local grammar school. The contents of the castle had long been dispersed, and the collections for the new museum in 1909 came from local people. These reflected the wealth of the town, principally as a producer of coal, in the golden era before the outbreak of the First World War, and were particularly strong in the fine and decorative arts. During its 1914 conference the Museums Association visited Cyfarthfa as an example of a modern museum and art gallery.

But for Merthyr Tudful, bad times were to come, and the slump of the 1920s and '30s was to hit the town particularly hard. Unemployment was a spectacular 80%; between 1921 and 1930, 12,000 jobs were lost, and 17,000 people left the town in the same decade. In no way could the local museum and art gallery develop in that time of human tragedy. It was underfinanced and inadequately manned, with the result that the museum until recently was a time capsule of pre-1914 museum techniques; the challenge to a now properly staffed museum is to preserve the old fashioned charm of the place whilst applying modern museum standards and presenting material in a thematic way.

The museum, with considerably extended premises in an historically important great house, is in the throes of development. The collections are extensive, and include art, archaeology, local and social history, natural history, geology, ethnology and, surprisingly, Egyptology. The fine art collection includes unique paintings of industrial scenes by the famous local artists Penry Williams (ill. on cover) and Thomas Prytherch, and an important collection of 20th century British art, particularly of Welsh origin, the paintings of Cedric Morris being especially impressive (colour plate 8). The museum has 400 oil paintings and 1000 watercolours, drawings and prints, whose display is rotated in the three art galleries. The decorative art collection of silver, china, porcelain, glass and furniture is also extensive. An interesting item are the thirty-four mid-Victorian brass instruments and a volume of original manuscript music of the Cyfarthfa Band, one of the numerous brass and silver bands that existed in Merthyr during its boom time.

Local and industrial history, including feats of achievement such as Richard Trevithick's pioneering locomotive run at nearby Abercynon, are interpreted in the Merthyr Room. Here are portraits of the Crawshay dynasty, and iron and steel samples that once decorated their boardroom. The political and social struggle of the people of Merthyr is not forgotten: there is a display on the Merthyr riots of 1831, and on the martyrdom of a local folk hero, Dic Penderyn, who was in the forefront of a radical movement in the town. Another famous hero, Keir Hardie, the first Labour MP elected to Parliament, is also remembered. It is planned to restore the Merthyr Room to its grandeur during the heyday of the Crawshays.

Inevitably, for a museum dealing with social history, there is yet another 'ye olde Welsh Kitchen', in this case a

Penry Williams, Interior view of Cyfarthfa Ironworks casting shed, *c. 1870 (one of a group of pictures commissioned by the Ironworks' owner)*

reconstruction of a Breconshire kitchen of about 1850.

The natural history gallery contains a collection of several hundred Edwardian stuffed birds and animals, many prepared by Mountney, the famous Brecon taxidermist. The geology collection has recently been re-displayed and contains important fossils relating to local coal measures. An unusual Egyptian collection was formed by H.H. Southey, a local army officer, whilst serving in the Middle East during the 1914–18 War. The museum's diverse ethnographic collection is also displayed here, and includes African spears, Persian armour, Russian samovars, Burmese boat models, Venetian enamelware, Norwegian skis, Japanese rooftiles, Nigerian bronzes and Indian playing cards!

The archaeological material includes Greek vases, Roman glass and Chinese celadon pottery, as well as finds made locally during excavations of the Roman fort at Penydarren.

A temporary exhibition gallery has recently been added, in which a wide range of changing displays are shown throughout the year.

A museum development plan has been adopted, which besides a massive conservation project, foresees an almost total re-display of the museum's collection. This will be possible through the creation of a range of galleries in the basement of the castle, which will virtually double the size of the museum. They will concentrate on social and industrial themes, covering the pre-industrial history of the area, as well as the iron, steel and coal trades that were so prominent.

The town of Merthyr Tudful, with its exciting story of rapid expansion followed by a period of unemployment, unrest and political agitation, has a great deal going for it. Its leisure and tourism facilities are being expanded, and the Merthyr Tudful Heritage Trust, together with the museum, is proceeding with an ambitious plan of conservation and presentation that can again bring prosperity, though of a different kind, to a town that has suffered greatly – socially, economically and culturally.

MILFORD HAVEN

Milford Haven Heritage & Maritime Museum

The Docks, Milford Haven, Dyfed
(06462) 3182

Open Mondays to Saturdays May to September. £

♿ S: wheelchair access to ground floor only; stairlift and wheelchair upstairs planned for future (check with museum).

🚻 & 👥 advisable to book in advance so a guide can be made available.

Milford Haven Heritage and Maritime Museum is in the process of moving from inadequate premises above a Masonic Hall to an old warehouse on Milford Docks, built in 1798 and probably the oldest building in the town. The museum is operated by a charitable Trust and receives a small grant from the Town Council. It is a museum in the making, and has the formidable task of interpreting the character of one of the most fascinating ports in Britain. Milford Haven had Royal Navy connections for a short while, attracted Quaker whaling families from Nantucket Island, and was one of the most important fishing ports in Britain. The aim of the museum is to collect material and interpret the unique history of the town. The museum has a good collection of tools used by the many tradesmen employed in ancillary trades to the trawling industry, such as shipwrights, blacksmiths, and sail and rope makers. The photographic collection relating to the history of the port is expanding, and there is also a small collection of Victorian dresses and items of furniture. At present, half of the ground floor at the new premises is open, with displays devoted to maritime subjects. It is hoped to put the rest of the museum's artefacts on

Aerial view of Milford Docks, c. 1935

Steam trawlers at Milford Docks in the 1920s

display in 1990, when the town's bicentenary will be celebrated.

The story of Milford as expounded in the museum is a fascinating one. In the late 18th century Sir William Hamilton, who had married into a local landowning family, proposed the building of a new town as a speculative venture. An Act of Parliament was obtained in 1790 and the building of the town of Milford began. A group of Quaker whalers from North America were persuaded to settle in the town, and the Royal Navy opened a shipbuilding yard in 1797. By 1815 both whalers and naval shipbuilders had ceased to operate from Milford, and the town became rather a shabby backwater. The coming of the railways in the 1840s revived the dreams of great-

World War II mine and a binnacle

ness: Milford was to be an important trans-Atlantic passenger port, for both the Manchester Railway and Brunel's South Wales railway were expected to terminate here. But the termini failed to materialise.

It was soon realised, however, that Milford's future lay in the fishing industry. Its proximity to the rich fishing grounds of the Western Approaches ensured that Milford was a boom town for many years. 'Every day a payday' was a common saying in the area. Ice-making plants and smoke houses for curing fish were set up on the dockside, and engineering and ship-repairing facilities were established to service the numerous trawlers and drifters using the port. At its peak some 2,000 people were employed in fishing

Some of the tools, documents, models and other items on display at Milford Haven museum

and its ancillary industries in and around Milford. The First World War marked a temporary setback, then the massive herring catches of the 1920s provided a tremendous impetus for the port's kippering trade. In 1932, the port possessed 108 of its own trawlers, with a further 150 vessels registered at other ports but based there for certain periods of the year. At that time Milford ranked as the fourth most important fishing port in Britain, after Hull, Grimsby and Fleetwood.

Without a doubt, the Milford Haven Heritage and Maritime Museum has an exciting and unusual story to tell, a story of Victorian enterprise and optimism, of the halcyon days when Milford was one of the greatest of British fishing ports.

MONMOUTH

Monmouth Museum (Nelson Collection and Local History Centre)

New Market Hall, Priory Street, Monmouth, Gwent NP5 3XA
(0600) 3519
Open daily except Sunday mornings. £ (ticket gives reduced admission to other Monmouth Borough Council museums).
♿ S: wheelchair access to ground floor only.
🚻 book in advance, reduced admission for pre-booked groups of 10 or more. 👥 F book in advance; children's worksheets available.

The Monmouth Borough Council administers four small museums within the county of Gwent – at *Abergavenny*, *Caldicot Castle*, **Chepstow** and Monmouth itself. Each one sets out to explore the history of the immediate locality of the museum; Monmouth also houses the Nelson Museum.

The local history collection at Monmouth traces the development of this Wye Valley town from its origins as a Roman border fortress and Norman settlement until more recent times. Displays of archaeological material from local excavations are under constant review because of continual development in the town centre. A special section commemorates the exploits of the Hon Charles Stewart Rolls – pioneer balloonist, aviator and motorist, and co-founder of Rolls-Royce. Paintings, prints and photographs are used to trace the growth of the town and the history of its buildings, the most famous of which is the Monnow Bridge Gate, a unique 13th-century survivor of the town's defences.

It was the mother of Charles Rolls, Lady Llangattock, who bequeathed an extensive collection of material associated with Admiral Nelson to the town

Lithograph after W.A. Overend, Nelson on the Quarterdeck of 'Victory' at Trafalgar

of Monmouth, near which she lived. The original Nelson Museum opened in 1924; further items have been added to the collection since. The wide variety of exhibits (colour plate 6) includes contemporary and later commemorative objects, especially pottery, silver and glass. Among the numerous relics are Nelson's fighting sword (the only one of his swords to have survived); many letters written by him, including ones to his wife and to Lady Hamilton; miniatures and logbooks; and prints and other items relating to his life, including his visit to Monmouth in 1802. There is also a collection of biographies and other relevant literature, and a range of small-scale memorabilia, including snuff boxes. A sample of the vast range of fake Nelsoniana is also displayed, including 'Nelson's glass eye'.

Monmouth Museum also stages regular temporary exhibitions on a variety of themes.

Abergavenny, a lively market town sixteen miles west of Monmouth, has had its small local museum since 1959. It is located within the ruins of the late medieval castle, in an extension of a 19th century Hunting Lodge built on the earth mound of the original Norman border fortress. After serving a variety of purposes this building was adapted between 1906 and 1961 for use as a museum. The contents relate mainly to the local history of Abergavenny. As a market town, Abergavenny supported a number of craftsmen who supplied the needs of an extensive agricultural hinterland, and the tools and equipment of a variety of these local trades are on view at the museum. The town was especially important for the manufacture of essentials for the horse age, and it is most appropriate that a display of tools and stock from the old saddler's shop of Williams and Son should form part of the main displays. Like most local museums, Abergavenny has accumulated a varied collection of artefacts, and a regularly changing selection from stored material is shown.

The Norman frontier castle at *Caldicot* has become well known as a venue for medieval banquets, held to the accompaniment of harps and singers. Restored in the 19th century, the castle now houses a museum collection of local history material. A small collection from Nelson's flagship, the 'Foudroyant', once owned by the castle's Victorian restorer, is also on show. Regular exhibitions are held of work by local artists and craftsmen. The castle's past is described in displays and a 'Soundalive' personal stereo guide. With its adjacent Country Park, which has gardens, play area, barbecue site, and plays host to various events, Caldicot Castle is one of the principal attractions of southern Gwent.

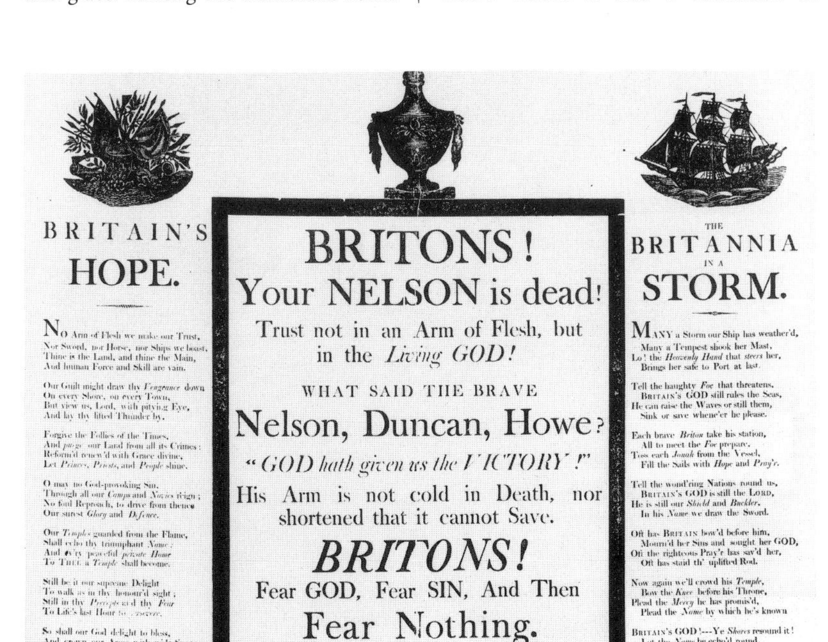

An evangelical poster printed shortly after Nelson's death

NEWPORT

Newport Museum and Art Gallery

John Frost Square, Newport, Gwent NP1 1HZ (0633) 840064
Closed Sundays. F ♿ W
& preferably book in advance; Schools Service – talks, workshops and loans scheme.
Tourist Information Centre.

Newport Museum and Art Gallery occupies a purpose-built modern building in the centre of the town. The entrance is in John Frost Square, named after a leader of the 1839 Chartist rising at Newport. Sharing a building with the public library, the museum contains material that illustrates the archaeology, natural history and social history of Gwent, together with a collection of mostly 19th and 20th century fine and decorative arts. Museum displays are arranged on the first and second floors, with the Art Gallery (where an extensive programme of temporary exhibitions is also shown) on the third floor. The museum celebrated its centenary in 1988 and displays are in the process of complete refurbishment.

There is an emphasis on Welsh and, more particularly, local artists in the collection of oil paintings, watercolours, drawings, prints and sculptures, while Newport's collection of English watercolours is an especially fine one and includes works by Dadd, Roberts and Rowlandson. As far as the decorative arts are concerned, the collection of teapots, Staffordshire figures and comemorative ware is an extensive one. A new teapot display, based on the gift of several hundred teapots by Mr John Wait, opened in 1989 and includes room settings, shop-window displays, and a range of tea advertisements and ephemera. Craft ceramics are well represented in the collection, since Gwent has a large number of talented studio potters living within its boundaries. The museum also has a collection of

Part of the Caerwent Bone Cave display

japanned ware produced by highly skilled workers in nearby **Pontypool**.

The archaeological collections at the museum are extensive. They range from prehistoric material (the oldest human footprints known from Britain, dating to around 6,000 BC, were found embedded in clay in the Severn Estuary near Newport) to items from the Middle Ages, but the bulk dates from the Roman period. A new permanent exhibition on Roman and prehistoric Newport opened in 1988. The most important group of finds is certainly that from the Roman town of Caerwent, a collection of international importance. This includes a number of inscribed and sculptured stones, a mosaic of the Four Seasons, and items relating to the structure of Roman dwellings, such as roof tiles, keys and door hinges. Bowls and jugs of Samian ware, bronze spoons and candlesticks are amongst the household effects, while brooches and pins, combs, rings, bracelets, and shoe and sandal soles illustrate articles of personal adornment and use. There are many examples of the agricultural and craft tools of the Roman period – mattock, bill-hooks, axes, sickles, hammers and planes, while amusements are represented by dice and other gaming counters. All in all, the Caerwent collection gives a fair indication of life in an important Roman town. Military items in the museum's collections came from the legionary fortress at **Caerleon**.

Newport is one of the great South Wales ports and an important centre of industry. 'The Making of Newport' exhibition covers local history to the end of the 19th century, with discoveries from medieval Newport, a selection of agricultural items, displays on coal mining, canals, the militia, and relics relating to John Frost and the unsuccessful Chartist uprising of 1839. Highlighted in particular are the port of Newport and the industrial and commercial development of the town in the 19th century. There are some fine ship models, and a nine-foot long working model of the famous Newport transporter bridge. The final section of these displays, taking the story further, is scheduled to open in 1991/92.

The natural sciences collections, of geological, botanical and zoological interest, are mostly of local material aimed at interpreting the landscape and natural life of south-east Wales. There are local rocks, fossils and minerals, as well as mounted specimens of birds and mammals, an herbarium, invertebrates, and fine collections of beetles (most of them from Essex) and of butterflies. The Gwent Biological Record Centre is based at the museum. New natural history displays, planned to open in 1990, will incorporate freshwater aquaria, wildlife in the home, and meteorology.

The collection of textiles is notable for its needlework samplers, a selection of which are shown. The museum also has costumes dating from the middle of the 19th century to the present day. Only a small selection of costumes and textiles is displayed; items in store can be seen by appointment.

Period room, c. 1800, in the 'Making of Newport' display

Sampler made in 1843

Tredegar House and Country Park

Newport, Gwent NP1 9YW
(0633) 62275
Open daily Good Friday to end of September (Country Park open all year). (to grounds only). W
& book in advance.

The opening of Tredegar House on the western outskirts of Newport in 1974 was one of the most significant events in the development of museums in Wales. Since that time, it has been gradually restored and refurbished as one of the finest country houses in the Principality. For five hundred years, Tredegar House was the home of the Morgan family, later the Lords of Tredegar, industrialists and entrepreneurs, who for centuries were the leaders of political and social life in Gwent. One wing of a medieval stone manor remains, but Tredegar House owes its character to the brick reconstruction of around 1670, when a series of stupendous rooms were included in the building. As the Morgan family grew richer during the 19th century a new servants' wing and service corridors were added to cope with the ever increasing needs of the family and their visitors. The Lords of Tredegar are no more, for with the departure of the last Lord of Tredegar to the tax haven of Monte Carlo in 1951, when the house was sold and its contents dispersed, the connection between Newport and its most influential aristocrats was severed. Tredegar House became a Catholic Girls Boarding School. In 1974 the house and grounds were put up for sale, for only the second time in 500 years, and it was purchased by Newport Borough Council, who set about the task of restoring and refurbishing Tredegar.

Although Tredegar House is an impressive mansion that once accommodated a 'grand' family, in its new guise as a local authority museum it is much more than yet another historic house open to the public. Of course, the house does contain a wealth of material relating to the privilege, power and influence of the Morgan family, from Llewellyn ap Morgan in 1402, to John, the last Lord Tredegar, who died in 1962; paintings and photographs of family members, from the worthy to the eccentric, are on display in the house. Twenty-five rooms are now open to the public (by guided tour) and the carefully refurbished interiors contain many fine pieces of furniture. The Brown Room, with lavishly carved oak panelling, and the richly decorated Gilt Room are two particularly striking interiors. Both house and contents provide an illuminating picture of some of

The north-west façade of Tredegar House, showing the wrought-iron gates made by William and Simon Edney of Bristol, 1714–18

The Still Room, where preserves, biscuits and household necessities were made by the Still Room maids

its residents. The so-called King's Room, for example, refurbished in the 1930s by Evan, Viscount Tredegar, was designed to accommodate one of the many altars that he erected around the house. As a young man Evan became a Roman Catholic, and Chamberlain to the Pope (an appointment that necessitated his presence in Rome for a month every year). But despite his faith, he still dabbled in black magic, and Tredegar House was a venue for a curious mixture of people attending wild and notorious weekend parties. They were kept entertained not only by Evan but by the menagerie of animals that he kept. The animals were as talented and eccentric as their master – the kangaroo, for example, boxed as well as hopped.

In addition to showing the lifestyle of an aristocratic family, Tredegar House contains a substantial section devoted to life 'below stairs'. In such a grand house there were as many rooms below stairs as there were above; in 1911, for instance, the house kept as many as twenty-two servants, not including those who came in to work every day. Today, the visitor is able to see the Great Kitchen with all its utensils and furniture, the Game Larder and Pastry Room, the Butler's Pantry, and the huge Servants' Hall that was the uncomfortable, cheerless home for so many of the staff of a great house.

Like most country houses, Tredegar had a substantial estate; ninety acres of the original 1,000 remain today. This included gardens, landscaped parkland

The Gilt Room, with imitation walnut panelling and gilded carving

The Blue Room, refurnished as a 20th century 'country house' interior

and the Home Farm, which together provided all the essential food and services for both family and servants, so that the estate community was virtually self-sufficient. The Home Farm buildings, clustered near the rear service entrance to Tredegar House, range in date from the early 17th to the 20th centuries. They can be visited as part of the Home Farm Trail. The old implement sheds, once used for the storage of farm machinery, have been converted to craft workshops. A number of craftsmen are based here and demonstrate their skills – pottery, glass-engraving, musical instrument-repairing, weaving – as well as selling their work to the visiting public. Other farm buildings that can be seen include the Stables (currently providing workspace for a silk weaver), the Mill, the Lesser Barn, the Greater Barn, the Cattlebyre, now housing shop and Information Centre, and the Brewhouse, now housing refreshment rooms.

The 17th century Stable Block, with its Orangery, is a delight, and perhaps the most impressive of the many outbuildings that surround the house. Visitors can also follow a Country Park Trail, beginning in the Sunken Garden, laid out in the 1930s, and continuing to the Lake and surrounding woodland, avenue, recently re-established hay meadow, and pond. A taped 'Soundalive' personal stereo tour to the formal gardens of the house, once the finest walled gardens in Wales, also describes the development of house and estate, and events and characters from Tredegar's past.

With its parkland, boating lake, an adventure play farm, and even carriage and donkey rides, Tredegar House and Country Park provides an ideal venue for an interesting day out. During the summer Tredegar House hosts a number of special events in the Park, which range from Horse Shows to Antique Fairs. Undoubtedly the most important of all was the housing of Wales' national festival – The Royal National Eisteddfod – in the grounds during the summer of 1988.

NEWTOWN

Newtown Textile Museum

5–7 Commercial Street, Newtown, Powys (0686) 26243
Open Easter week, and Whitsun weekend to 30 September, Mondays to Saturdays. F
♿ S: access for disabled/infirm very difficult.
🚻 & 👥 pre-book in writing to Curator.

The museum, established as a private museum in 1967 (and now in the process of being taken over by Powys County Council), occupies the third and fourth floors of an old flannel-weaving factory in what was once the most important of all Welsh textile-producing towns. To the travellers who came to Wales in the early 19th century, Newtown, or to give its proper name, Llanfair-yng Nghedewain, was 'the Leeds of Wales', which witnessed an amazing development between 1790

Exterior view, Newtown Textile Museum

Louvre boards, doorway and window salvaged from buildings in Newtown

Hand cards

and 1850. The wool textile industry, producing flannel mainly for an export market, depended very heavily on hand-loom weavers, for it was not until the 1850s that power looms were introduced on any scale. 'The power loom does not work without the tenderness of a skilful human hand', said a contemporary writer. It was a great advantage for hand-loom weavers to locate their shops as near as possible to the source of raw material, that is the carding and spinning factories, which since the early years of the 19th century were located on the river banks, close to their source of water power. Although a certain amount of weaving continued to be carried out in the remote cottages and farmhouses of rural Powys, a factory system gradually developed in the weaving industry, especially in Newtown. The Textile Museum occupies one of these factories, established in the 1830s in one of the principal working streets of this important textile manufacturing town. Tall, three or four-floored buildings such as this, with their numerous windows, continue to bear witness to the importance of wool in the history of Powys. A weaving factory would occupy perhaps the third or fourth floors of a building stretched above a number of cottage dwellings, generally of the back-to-back variety. The factory was usually entered by an outside staircase at the back of the terrace.

The displays in this authentic building are concerned with tracing the history of the wool textile industry from its early beginnings in the late 16th century to its demise during the last quarter of the 19th century. On some days there are demonstrations of hand carding, spinning and hand-loom weaving, and the collection of textile tools and equipment is supported by an extensive one of photographs and documents relating to the most important of Welsh rural industries. One interesting aspect of the textile industry explored in the museum is the establishment of the first mail order business in the world, Pryce Jones's store, by a Newtown businessman in the 1860s. That business, with world-wide contacts, employed over 300 people in its heyday, but it was a venture based entirely on the sale of 'Real Welch flannel direct from the looms, Gentleman's Welch Tweeds, Shawls, Blankets, Hosiery and sterling value clothing for the poor'.

Closely related to the wool textile industry was that of leather production, an industry that still flourishes in the Newtown area. The tools of leather tanning are on display at the museum, as are those of the fellmonger, who was concerned with the processing of sheepskins and the production of skin wool for the woollen industry.

The Newtown Textile Museum, located in an historically important building, is a successful private venture that interprets an activity that was of vital importance in ordering the lives of past generation of mid-Wales people.

PEMBROKE

Museum of Gypsy Caravans

Commons Road, Pembroke, Dyfed
(0646) 631308
Open Easter to September,
Mondays to Fridays and Sundays.

& welcome; information packs for schools.

Close to the walls of the impressive Castle at Pembroke was a tanyard that had lain derelict for many years. In the 1970s, however, an enthusiastic collector of all manner of artefacts associated with gypsy crafts and gypsy lore set about the task of establishing a national collection of gypsy wagons, and Mr Alistair Campbell has adapted the old tanyard buildings to accommodate a first-class collection relating to gypsies. It has been a one-man, under-financed effort, but its owner has the advantage of being a competent craftsman with the ability to restore the large number of vehicles in his care. Of course, restoration is a slow process, demanding skills in wheelwrighting, coach building and painting, and although there are many living caravans and vending carts at the museum that are in dire need of restoration, there are others that have been fully restored to their original condition. They display the bright and complex decoration associated with such vehicles, and most are fully furnished as living caravans.

The types of caravan here range from a canvas bow-topped vehicle, with highly decorated undercarriage and body, to a much larger wagon with clerestory skylight on the roof. The best-known of all gypsy wagons was the so-called Reading van, which was regarded as the most luxurious of all gypsy vehicles. The prototype was made by Dunton of Reading, although vehicles of the same type were made in other parts of the country. The Reading wagon was large and cumbersome, and rarely made an appearance in the hillier parts of the country. It was a vehicle usually ordered by wealthy horse dealers and the upper crust of Romany society.

Interior view of a Square Bow Wagon, c. 1930

Although the most spectacular part of the collection at the museum in Pembroke consists of a variety of caravans in various stages of restoration, the other activities of gypsies are not ignored. Various Romany crafts, such as artificial flower making and clothes-peg making, as well as tinsmithing are also represented. The crafts of blacksmithing and wheelwrighting, together

Rod Tent

Interior of restored Ledge Board Wagon built by H. Jones, Hereford, 1895

Exterior of restored Ledge Board Wagon

with the wide range of tools used in those crafts, are displayed and demonstrated, as is the craft of coach painting and the preparation of hand-ground paint. The museum has an active policy of collecting relevant material, especially that relating to the art of tinsmithing, which was of considerable importance in Romany life.

The Gypsy Museum is obviously undermanned and under-financed, but as a unique museum in the Principality its development should be encouraged, for it deals with a group of people whose history is not well interpreted in any other institution. Despite winning a Prince of Wales award and a Certificate of Merit from the British Tourist Authority, the museum may be in danger of closing.

PENARTH

Turner House

Plymouth Road, Penarth, South Glamorgan CF6 2DH
(0222) 708870
Closed lunchtimes, Sunday mornings and all day Mondays. £
♿ W: wheelchair access to ground floor only.
🚻 & 👫 welcome.

Penarth is a seaside town at the south end of Cardiff Bay, which is being rapidly transformed with the revitalisation programme being undertaken by the Cardiff Bay Development Corporation. In the late 19th and early years of the 20th century, Penarth reigned supreme as a modest, respectable seaside resort, with promenade, pier, and a few seaside attractions. It had a dock that in the heyday of the South Wales coal trade flourished, exporting coal to all parts of the world until its closure in the 1930s. But that coal dock was well hidden from the respectable streets of Penarth Heights, which really served as a dormitory area for Cardiff. Penarth was, for many years, a town greatly favoured by the shipowners and businessmen of Cardiff as their home; indeed, one street of Victorian houses overlooking the sea was known as 'Millionaire's Row'.

Interior view, Turner House

Exterior view, Turner House

Interior view of the first-floor galleries

One of those wealthy businessmen, James Pyke Thompson, set up an art gallery in the town in memory of the artist J.M.W. Turner in 1888. It was a philanthropic venture intended to interest the public in the type of art that Pyke Thompson himself would have collected. The collection of paintings, ceramics, enamels, prints and watercolours was at first housed in a gallery attached to Thompson's home, but in due course his house was demolished and the gallery was enlarged. Fortunately for Penarth, the Turner House Gallery was taken over in 1921 by the **National Museum of Wales** as a branch of its department of art, and has continued as such to the present day. Without that development it could have become a fossil, yet another memorial interpreting the taste of its original benefactor and nothing more. In 1946 the small red-brick building, near the centre of Penarth, assumed its present form, with further improvements added in the early 1980s.

The Turner House Gallery does not have collections of its own, but items of furniture and china from the National Museum's collections are always on view there, and form an almost permanent background to the art and other exhibitions staged in the gallery throughout the year. Local art societies are regularly offered opportunities to exhibit their members' work, usually for sale, and although most of the exhibitions organised are art-orientated other disciplines within the National Museum of Wales are occasionally represented. An exhibition of Welsh oak furniture from the collections of the **Welsh Folk Museum**, for example, proved very popular, while another, drawing on the collections of the **Welsh Industrial and Maritime Museum** and illustrating the history of Penarth as a port, proved to be of considerable local interest. Nevertheless it is fine and applied art for which the original gallery was designed, and this aspect dominates the exhibition programme of Turner House; for that reason it may not be as popular with the residents of Penarth as other aspects of the cultural history of Wales could be.

PONTERWYD

Llywernog Silver-Lead Mine and Museum

Ponterwyd, Aberystwyth, Dyfed SA46 0AU (0970) 85620
Open daily Easter to October.
♿ ST: partial wheelchair access – mine workings lie on a hillside; no access to Balcombes Level.
& preferably book in advance: contact Curator.

l to r, Jigger shed, Eagle Foundry water-wheel, Museum entrance, Main building

Lead, like tin, has been mined and quarried in Britain for some 2,000 years, and it is only within the last half-century or so that it has ceased to be worked as cheaper foreign ores have become increasingly available. Closely associated with lead was the mining of silver, and Llywernog mine, opened as a museum of the industry, was as much a silver mine as it was a lead one. The area around the remote village of Ponterwyd, eleven miles east of Aberystwyth, was a particularly rich area for both lead and silver, and an exhibition of mining within the museum complex is rightly entitled 'The California of Wales' (taking its name, in fact, from a small mine that existed in the Llywernog Valley in the 1850s). An imaginative picture of underground workings has been recreated here, and to give the visitor a better understanding of the life and toils of a mining community a short tape-slide programme is presented at regular intervals.

The story of lead and silver mining, as it unfolds at the Llywernog Museum, is an exciting and romantic one. Central Wales, an area of lonely, rolling hills, was not always a rural backwater, and not all the pursuits of its people were associated with tilling the land and breeding animals, for the area saw the development of a very important non-ferrous metal complex. The port of Aberystwyth was developed specifically for the export of the metallic ores that were extracted from dozens of mines whose remains still dot the landscape. Although lead ore was extracted in Roman times, it was during the reign of Queen Elizabeth I, with the foundation of the Society of the Mines Royal, that the industry developed. People like Sir Hugh Middleton made a huge profit from the extraction of lead and silver ore, while in 1637 another entrepreneur, Thomas Bushell, was given the right to mint silver coin at Aberystwyth. That enterprise was stopped by Oliver Cromwell when he destroyed Aberystwyth Castle in 1647, and for the remainder of the 17th century little ore was extracted. With the formation of the Mines Adventurers Company in 1690, however, the lead and silver mining industries were to flourish tremendously, and in the 18th century northern Ceredigion became one of the most productive mining regions in Britain. Cornish miners migrated to the remote hills of central Wales by the hundreds, and brought with them their own brand of Wesleyan Methodism which still dominates religious life in the villages of the region. A village such as Ponterwyd witnessed the equivalent of a gold rush, and the period of prosperity continued unabated until the end of the 19th century. Unfortunately, cheap ore from Spain, North America and Australasia then flooded the market, and the non-ferrous metal industry that had brought so much prosperity to a remote corner of Wales declined very rapidly.

Main engine-shaft and headframe

An industry that was of such vital importance in the economic life of Wales for such a long period of time is indeed worthy of a full interpretation. The coal industry and the slate-quarrying industry have had their museums and their preserved sites for many years, and those industries are fully represented in perhaps too many locations. Llywernog remains the only institution devoted to the study of a very important industry; as such it has made, and is making, a very valuable contribution to the visitor's appreciation of an industry not usually associated with a remote rural area. Here, at this small but once prolific mine, one can follow a way marked 'Miner's Trail', which tells the exciting story of silver and lead mining in Wales. The visitor can also go underground into Balcombe's level and see a floodlit cavern containing the Blue Pool, a prospecting pit sunk around 1795. Other fascinating exhibits on this six-acre site include the 1870 Counting House, a rock-crusher house, an engine shaft and headframe, water wheels, a horse whim and a powder house. A 50ft-diameter water-wheel awaits restoration, hopefully to begin in 1990. Work on restoring the enormous wheel-pit on the site has recently been carried out. The wheel was originally used in a lead mine on the Isle of Man, but was sold to a china clay-mining company on Bodmin Moor when the lead mine was shut down following an underground calamity. It was brought to Wales in 1976 by courtesy of the Trevithick Society and when restored will form the central feature of Llywernog Museum.

Eagle Foundry Water-wheel, with Cardigan Foundry Water-wheel in the distance

A group visiting Balcombe's level, a prospecting tunnel dug c. 1795

The Llywernog Silver-Lead Mine provides information on the remains of many other mines of northern Ceredigion and south-west Powys, and for those with a special interest a visit to other mining settlements in the area is worthwhile. Not far away, for example, is the Cwmsymlog mine, developed in the early 1600s to provide silver for the royal coffers, while the lunar-like landscape of Cwmystwyth provides evidence of the very flourishing extractive industry that was once of such great importance in that ghost village. Ystymtuen, which lies atop the ridge south of the Llywernog Valley, sits on the remains of a string of mines of the Castell Lode. This village includes a Wesleyan Methodist chapel of enormous proportions, a post office and a primary school (now housing a Youth Hostel). The shafts at Llywernog came up to the ground within yards of the houses in some places. Not far from Llywernog is another desolate village, Dylife, whose productive mine was once owned by Cobden and Bright, while nearby are the Van lead mines, said to have been the most profitable lead mines in mid-Wales.

PONTYPOOL

The Valley Inheritance Museum (Torfaen Museum Trust)

Park Buildings, Pontypool, Gwent NP4 6JH (04955) 52036
Closed Sunday mornings. W & book in advance with Visitor Services Unit.

The Valley Inheritance Museum, Pontypool, is housed in the former stables of Pontypool Park House, once the mansion of the Hanbury family who from the late 17th century laid the foundation for industrial growth in the Pontypool area. Gwent's Eastern Valley, stretching from **Blaenafon** in the north, through Pontypool, Abersychan and Cwmbran, to Llantarnam in the south, was an area of intense industrial activity. The technological innovations of the Hanbury family of Pontypool in the iron and tinplate industries, and their manufacture of japanned ware in particular, brought considerable prosperity to a town that was amongst the first in Wales to experience industrialisation. Much of the rich heritage of the Eastern Valley survives to the present day in the form of sites of ironworks, canals, coal mines, and workers' houses, and the Valley Inheritance at Pontypool Park is an excellent introduction to an exploration of this fascinating valley. 'The Torfaen Trail of History' has as its motto 'Where Yesterdays make for Great Todays', and from the Blaenafon Iron Works and **Big Pit Mining Museum** to the modern planned town of Cwmbran, the valley has much to offer.

The stable block that accommodates the 'Valley Inheritance' exhibition was erected in the 1830s, and contained accommodation for horses and carriages as well as tack rooms, storage and hay lofts. The stalls were in constant use until 1915, when the last squire of Pontypool, John Hanbury, died. For the next fifty years or so the beautifully proportioned stables were used for a variety of purposes, ranging from a disinfectant works to a barracks for Sikh soldiers. In 1978, however, they were taken over by the Torfaen Museum Trust, which continued a programme of repairs and rehabilitation begun by the Torfaen Borough Council in 1975. Although the exterior was restored to its original character, the interior was adapted to provide modern facilities for exhibitions on the development of Torfaen and its people. The work was completed in 1980,

The Georgian stable block now housing the Valley Inheritance Museum

Pontypool Japanned ware tray, probably made c. 1781–1811

Road repairing in Commerical Street, Pontypool, c. 1930

and the centre was opened in May 1981. Within the building, exhibits, photographs and an audio-visual presentation describe the life of the people who lived in the Eastern Valley of Gwent, and the exhibits recall the contribution made by past communities to the industrial prosperity of South Wales. The centre produces its own lively newsletter, *Outreach*, and a number of publications that provide the visitor with an appreciation of the rich industrial heritage of south-east Wales. Above all, the museum is a starting point for an exploration of Gwent's Eastern Valley, and the Trust itself runs two significant sites, which are of importance in interpreting the area.

The first of these sites is Junction Cottage at Pontymoel, built in 1814 at the junction of two waterways – the Monmouthshire Canal, and the Brecknock and Abergavenny Canal. Junction Cottage once housed a lock-keeper, whose main responsibility was not to raise and lower barges but to supervise locks that were designed to restrict the movement of water from the Brecknock and Abergavenny to the Monmouthshire, for each company jealously guarded its water supply. The two companies were not amalgamated until 1865. The cottage now houses an exhibition that tells the story of the local waterways system, which was of crucial importance to the industrial development of south-east Wales. Near Junction Cottage is an impressive aqueduct, which represents a fine example of canal engineering.

Metal casting at GKN in Cwmbran

The Torfaen Museum Trust was instrumental in saving a very important row of twelve workers' cottages at Forge Row, Cwmafon. These cottages, now utilised as dwellings, are probably the best examples of early 19th century industrial housing in South Wales. Another major project has been the renovation of Llanyrafon Farm, Cwmbran, as the Trust's museum of local agricultural life. This 18th century manor house is being fully restored, as are the grounds and the farmstead. Located as it is in the newest of Welsh towns, it reminds the visitor that Gwent is not just an industrial region with little else to offer. For despite its industrial heart, Gwent possesses a beautiful countryside, where crop and animal husbandry is still the main occupation of its people.

PONTYPRIDD

Pontypridd Historical and Cultural Centre

Bridge Street, Pontypridd, Mid Glamorgan CF37 4PE
(0443) 402077/480786
Closed Sundays and Mondays. ■ ■
■ W
book in advance, ■.

Tabernacl, the old chapel now housing the Historical and Cultural Centre

Miners lamps, c. 1760 to modern

The market town of Pontypridd is located at the confluence of the Rivers Taff and Rhondda, and has always been regarded as the 'capital' of Wales' most heavily industrialised valleys. Its development as a commercial centre began with the opening in 1795 of the 25 mile long Glamorganshire Canal between Cardiff Docks and Merthyr Tudful, which really opened up the valleys to intensive industrialisation.

A notable feature of all Welsh valley towns were the large nonconformist chapels that catered for the spiritual needs of a rapidly expanding population in the 19th century. Those chapels are a dominant feature of the urban landscape of the mining valleys, though many have long since ceased to be places of worship. It was in such a building – Tabernacl – in the centre of Pontypridd that the Historical and Cultural Centre was opened in 1986. The chapel was built in 1861, and was magnificently refurbished in 1910, but ceased to be a place of worship in 1983. In creating the Centre, the character of the original building has been preserved. The highly decorated ceiling has been restored to its former glory while the pulpit, the 'big seat' that once accommodated the deacons, and the highly ornate pipe-organ provide a compelling focal point.

The presentation of local history is an important part of the Centre's function, and one of several photographic exhibitions explores the theme of Pontypridd as the 'Gateway of the Valleys'. The coal industry in the area is traced in detail within the exhibition, while some of the better known local industries, such as the Brown Lennox Chain Factory, are also represented. The latter factory, which still exists, provided chains for ships in Nelson's time, and also for some of Brunel's great steamships. In addition, eminent local figures, from Dr William Price, the pioneer of cremation, to Sir Geraint Evans, the famous opera singer, and even Tom Jones, Pontypridd's most internationally famous son, are all featured in the exhibition. The words and music of the Welsh National Anthem, 'Hen Wlad fy Nhadau' (Land of my Fathers) were written by Evan James (1809–1878) and his son John James

(1832–1902), who were weavers in the town. Three-dimensional objects are gradually being acquired to supplement the various flat-board exhibitions in the museum.

The Centre houses a substantial collection of miners' lamps, which includes traditional oil lamps, early battery-operated lamps, and modern-day cap lights. Within the last few years the coal mining industry in the Rhondda and Taff Valleys has been totally obliterated, but the collection reminds the visitor of this industry's importance as one of the foremost activities that drew labour from all parts of the world to the once flourishing valleys.

An important and expanding part of the Centre is devoted to an exhibition on Chapels in Wales. By tradition, Pontypridd is a fiercely nonconformist town, and it is only natural that an exhibition located in a first class example of a valley chapel should be devoted to a representation of Welsh places of worship. Though more fortunate than many, Tabernacl in Pontypridd is one of an increasing number of chapels that no longer serve as places of worship. Some have found new uses; others fall into disrepair, eventually to be demolished, and thus a very characteristic feature of the Welsh landscape is in danger of being lost. 'The Chapels of Wales' is a major theme explored at the Pontypridd Historical and Cultural Centre. There is an active programme of recording details of both urban and rural chapels, and their plans and photographs are displayed here. From the simplest, most basic building, to the most elaborate structures of the early 20th century, the ever-changing exhibition is a fascinating one.

Part of the Centre is devoted to monthly exhibitions of art, photography and craft work by local societies and schools, and there is also a programme of visiting exhibitions from other museums and organisations.

One fascinating feature adjacent to the Centre is Pontypridd's most famous landmark, the Old Bridge, built in 1756. When it was built, this was the longest single-span bridge in Europe, and attracted attention and fame from far and wide.

PORTHMADOG

Porthmadog Maritime Museum

Greaves Wharf, Porthmadog
Gwynedd (0766) 573736
(enquiries to *Mr Eifion Davies, Gowerian, Ralph Street, Borth-y-gest, Porthmadog, Gwynedd (0766) 572864*)
Open Easter week, and May Bank Holiday to end of September, otherwise by appointment. £ P
♿: wheelchair access to museum but not to lifeboat.
🚻 & 👥 preferably book in advance.

William Maddocks

In North Wales a series of harbours were developed specially for the export of the region's main product – slates. Of all these ports, probably the most important and fascinating is Porthmadog. Built by William Maddocks in the early 19th century, the town developed not only as an important slate-exporting port, but also as one of the principal shipbuilding centres of the west coast of Wales. The beautiful three-masted schooners that came from the shipyards of Porthmadog, known to contemporaries as 'Western Ocean Yachts', gained an enviable reputation for speed and grace. In the 19th century they took slate to Scandinavia and the Baltic; they were engaged in the salt-fish trade of Newfoundland and Labrador; they sailed to South America and the Carribean, and to Australia and the Far East. The small well-planned Gwynedd town from

The crew of the Porthmadog ship, 'Moel Tryvan'

which the ships and sailors originated was in every sense a maritime community that looked outwards to the world. This exciting story of achievement is told in the Porthmadog Maritime Museum, which quite rightly has found a home on one of the old slate wharves of Porthmadog Harbour. In the only remaining slate shed, there is a fascinating display on the maritime history of the town, and the story of the local shipbuilders and seafarers is told in the context of the general history of seafaring in Gwynedd.

Painting of a Porthmadog ship

In the exhibition, particular reference is placed on wreck and rescue, for Porthmadog was described as 'a nasty corner of a nasty bay', and the continually changing approach channels to the port always made navigation difficult. The former Barmouth lifeboat, the 'Chieftain', is on display at the museum. There are plans at Porthmadog to construct a new purpose-built museum, but in the meantime exhibition space in what was, after all, a slate storage shed is very limited. Nevertheless, the museum is able to present a story that can serve as a starting point to an exploration of a unique maritime settlement, which has a great deal to offer.

The steep hillside near the harbour was the first area to be developed. In 1825 there were only a dozen houses, but by 1850 there were 200. Here were the rope walks, where in narrow open-air corridors ropemakers twisted the long lengths of hemp to provide ropes for sailing vessels; here, too, were the sail lofts, where the enormous sheets of canvas sails were cut and stitched. Near the harbour were the offices of the Porthmadog Ship Insurance Society, established in Cornhill in 1841. This was an extremely influential organisation, which insured most of the Porthmadog ships and enforced high standards of both seafaring and shipbuilding. Cornhill also had its thriving navigation school, where the sailors of the town learned their trade. Since exports from Porthmadog exceeded imports, many ships arrived at Porthmadog in ballast, and that ballast of sand and stones from many parts of the world was dumped on a sandy site at the mouth of the River Glaslyn. An island gradually developed here, and the Ballast Bank, with its varied flora, is a notable feature of the landscape.

Porthmadog would not have developed at all were it not for the building of a long embankment, 'The Cob', by William Maddocks in 1811, which formed part of a massive land reclamation scheme. The Cob not only carried a roadway but also the lines of the Ffestiniog narrow-gauge railway, now a tourist facility but once the lifeline that brought the slates of *Blaenau Ffestiniog* to its exporting port. The small *Ffestiniog Railway Museum* at the Porthmadog railway terminus traces the history of this, one of the earliest railway companies in Britain (it was opened on April 1st, 1836). The early transport of slate was by horse, cart and river, in lighters down the River Dwyryd to the ocean-going craft waiting in the bay. The tramroad built by Maddocks during the construction of the Cob embankment was the forerunner of the famous Ffestiniog Railway.

Maritime museums are an area of growth in the development of museum services in Wales, and in addition to Porthmadog, the county of Gwynedd already possesses maritime collections in *Holyhead,* **Caernarfon**, *Barmouth* and *Nefyn*, with many others being

A Ffestiniog Railway locomotive

proposed or planned. But it is certainly not enough to place a few artefacts in glass cases, stick a few pictures of ships in full sail on the wall, and call the place a 'maritime museum', as has been done in so many locations. A maritime museum, located on the edge of the land beside the sea, has far more to do than preserve the nostalgia of a bygone age. It must look to the hinterland from which it drew its wealth; the maritime museum at Porthmadog, for example, means very little if it does not tell the story of Ffestiniog slates. In addition, a maritime museum has to look at the coastal settlement that it represents, at the story of its people and its ships. But far more importantly, it must look outwards to lands beyond the sea, to where its ships and seamen travelled. Thus, the connection of Porthmadog with Hamburg and other Baltic ports is an aspect of maritime history that was of vital importance in the development of the port, and an aspect that needs to be explored further within the museum. A typical trading pattern for the Porthmadog Western Ocean Yacht between about 1880 and the outbreak of the First World War in 1914 was to take slates from Porthmadog to Hamburg, then to carry German goods to the Mediterranean; it would then carry a cargo of wine and other Mediterranean products to Newfoundland, and return from there to Britain with a cargo of salt fish or timber.

Porthmadog is a fascinating town, which has much to show of its past glory as a seafaring community. In such a community, maritime activity was all embracing, claiming to a greater or lesser extent the time and interest of the majority of its inhabitants. Times have changed, and the intensity of Wales' maritime connections is but a shadow of what it was half a century ago. The decline of commercial activity in such a port as Porthmadog has been rapid and spectacular, and a tradition has died. That tradition needs more effective interpretation and recording than that provided at present by the modest Porthmadog Maritime Museum and the other small museums of coastal Wales.

RHYL

Rhyl Museum

Church Street, Rhyl, Clwyd
LL18 3AA (0352) 2121
Open daily. F P W
& preferably book in advance.

Rhyl Museum is a new venture, having been opened as part of the new Library, Museum and Arts Centre in May 1986. Situated in the centre of this somewhat brash seaside resort, this building accommodates an extensive library, community rooms for use by local societies and groups, and a major gallery area equipped to display exhibitions of national and international stature. Above the gallery on the first floor is a local museum, which is being developed to show Rhyl's maritime and tourist heritage. The gallery has been designed to resemble the now demolished Rhyl pier, and features a mural depicting the promenade at the turn of the century. In addition to a display of artefacts there are two video presentations in the museum, using early movie films to present the atmosphere of one of Wales' most important seaside resorts.

The collection of artefacts, although small as yet, has been built up through the generosity of local people. One of the most interesting aspects of the collection is the large number of porcelain souvenirs, many dating back to the Edwardian era when Rhyl was developing as a seaside resort. The town itself was certainly a creation of late 19th and early 20th century tourism; its pier, with concert hall seating 2000 people, was built in 1867, and a full programme of entertainment was organised for its visitors. On August Bank Holiday in 1896, for example, 'Aquatic entertainments' were organised on the pier; 'Songs and Sketches' were organised at the Pier Pavilion; minstrels sang on the beach; the operetta group was flourishing, and the town band played on the promenade.

Model of the Rhyl lifeboat, 'Caroline Richardson'

The museum's mural depicting Rhyl around 1910

Plays were performed in the town hall, and 'animated photographs' were shown in the Winter Gardens. Throughout the present century Rhyl has held its own as the principal seaside resort on the North Wales coast, and the story of its development, spanning little more than a hundred years, is interpreted in its local museum.

Although the town itself is of fairly recent origin, and was created through the popularity of seaside holidays, the maritime and seafaring traditions of the Clwyd estuary go back for many centuries. That maritime tradition is another theme explored in Rhyl museum. A small port at Foryd in the estuary was in constant use until the 1930s, mainly for the importation of timber. The museum has an interesting movie of a Rhyl lifeboat that served a section of the North Wales coast from 1897 to 1937. The 'Caroline Richardson' was a tubular boat designed by Messrs. Richardson of Aberhirnant, Bala, and constructed by the Thomas Iron Works, Black Wall, at a cost of £548. The vessel was the last tubular lifeboat in service. An early film of the launching and retrieving of the boat may be viewed at the museum, while some of the original fittings of the boat, including an oar and sails, are also on display.

As with many other Welsh museums, that at Rhyl is in the early stages of development. Its collections have only been assembled recently, but its small exhibition area, exploring the tourism, maritime and civic heritage of the town, is both pleasant and informative. Future plans include displays on the social history of Rhyl.

Part of a temporary exhibition in the art gallery

RHYMNEY VALLEY

Rhymney Valley District Council Museum Service

Ystrad Fawr, Ystrad Mynach, Hengoed, Mid Glamorgan CF8 7SF (0443) 815588 ext. 221
Projects currently underway are due to open as follows:
Bute Town – Spring 1990; seasonal opening.
Caerphilly, Central Museum – Spring 1992; will be open all year.
Llancaiach Fawr – Summer 1991; will be open all year.
New Tredegar, Elliot Colliery – Spring 1991; seasonal opening.
Tir Trosnant, Craft workshops – Summer 1989; open all year.
Tir Trosnant, Interpretation Centre – Summer 1993; will be open all year.
Check with Museums Service for up-to-date information.
£ ♿ W (except Llancaiach Fawr which ♿ S, wheelchair access to ground floor only)

The Rhymney Valley in Mid-Glamorgan, once a vibrant industrial valley, is now amongst the most deprived in Great Britain, with an unacceptably high rate of unemployment, and housing conditions that are among the worst in the country. Yet this valley, which on the face of it is a typical derelict area that has witnessed rapid de-industrialisation, has much of interest to those concerned with the heritage of South Wales. Caerphilly Castle in the south of the valley is amongst the best preserved of all Welsh castles, described by one writer as being 'unsurpassed in Britain', while the northern boundaries of the valley in the Brecon Beacons have much to offer the natural historian.

Llancaiach Fawr, looking north west

It was only within the last four years that the potential of the Rhymney Valley began to be appreciated when the local authority and its Public Relations Unit prepared a full-scale survey of what might be possible in the development of a heritage project within the valley. Much work needs to be done and the development depends very much on the availability of funds, but work on setting up a series of related museums is currently underway.

At the extreme westward side of the Rhymney District area, the refurbishment of a 16th century farmhouse, Llancaiach Fawr House, sited alongside the B4254 road, is virtually complete. This house, a Grade I listed building, survived almost unaltered from the 16th century and is regarded as being one of the most important and exciting survivals in Glamorgan. It was closely associated with the Prichard family, one member of which was a leader of the Civil War in South Wales. With the development of the house as an interpretative centre, Llancaiach Fawr can become a starting point and a springboard for tourism within the Rhymney Valley, especially for the introduction to visitors of the pre-industrial landscape.

Bute Town, at the top end of the Rhymney Valley, is a small village of restored workers' cottages of considerable importance. In 1801 the Union Ironworks were established in the valley, and the workers who migrated to the new works were accommodated in quickly-erected terraces of houses that became known as Bute Town. Although the terraces were to be the nucleus of a small, planned town, the ambitious project never reached fruition, and only three terraces were completed. With the restoration of the houses in 1974 as part of the European Architectural Heritage Year, the terraces are now fully-occupied dwellings, but two cottages are being developed as a small interpretative centre (due to open in Spring 1991). In one will be a reconstructed interior of the late 19th century, while the house next door is being adapted to create a museum of industrial-period domestic life in the Rhymney Valley.

The Elliot Colliery Winding House at New Tredegar is a preserved monument under the care of CADW and administered by the Rhymney Valley District Council. Work is proceeding on building an extension on two sides of the Winding House to accommodate displays relating to the industrial development of the Valley, in order to create a museum of labour and industry (scheduled to open in 1991), which will complement Bute Town. The engine, the last of its type in South Wales, is a very large twin-tandem compound steam-powered engine, constructed in 1891 for winding at the Powell Duffryn-owned colliery. But important though the preservation of a single engine of this kind may be, and interesting though it is to the technically minded, the engine house as it now stands looks incongruous in the middle of a reclaimed industrial desert. For the coal mine and its associated buildings and headgear were demolished soon after the closure of Elliot Colliery in 1967; the banks of terraced houses that surrounded it have all disappeared, and the network of railway lines that were once vital have all been lifted.

Bute Town village, middle and lower row

Among the other museum projects that are being furthered in the Rhymney Valley is the development of Tir Trosnant Farm at Gelligaer, which is currently being set up by Community Industry as a work experience centre for unemployed youths to learn the skills of animal husbandry and other aspects of country life. Craft workshops on the site opened in summer 1989 and a field centre concerned with the natural history and agricultural development of the valley is scheduled for 1993.

Elliot Colliery Winding House, with groundworks for the museum extension, left

A new purpose-built museum and heritage centre is planned for a site near Caerphilly Castle. This will house displays providing an introduction to the Rhymney Valley, as well as the museum service's central stores, administration, library and technical facilities. It is hoped that this Central Museum will be built by 1992.

In addition to the various sites in the care of the Rhymney Valley District Council Museums Service, there are several independent museum projects in the valley. Rhymney Museum has been established in the town of Rhymney, in an old Methodist Chapel in the care of the Rhymney Civic and Historical Society. The building has been renovated under a Community Programme scheme, with exhibition hall on the ground floor and provision for four craft workshops and an art gallery on the first floor, but as yet the museum has no collections. It is hoped to make it into a local community-based museum. Elsewhere a pre-industrial woollen mill, Ystrad Mill, is currently being restored by the Ystrad Mill Society and is scheduled to open in 1990. The Society plans to also create a visitor centre at the mill in the future.

SWANSEA

Glynn Vivian Art Gallery and Museum

Alexandra Road, Swansea, West Glamorgan SA1 5DZ
(0792) 655006/651738
Open daily. F
♿ ST: wheelchair access to ground floor via ramp in Sculpture Court; lift available to Main Gallery by prior appointment; balcony area only reached via steps but assistance will be given by attendants if possible.
book in advance if tours etc. required.
book in advance: contact Education Officer to book and for details of workshops etc.

Ceri Richards, Homage to Dylan Thomas, *1954*

In 1905, Richard Glynn Vivian, a copper manufacturer who accumulated great wealth from an industry that was of prime importance in the Swansea Valley, offered money to Swansea Corporation to build an art gallery. Oddly enough the Corporation, who were nervous of the costs of maintenance and staffing, did not immediately accept the offer, and it was not until 1909 that the foundation stone of the Glynn Vivian Art Gallery was laid by Glynn Vivian, who unhappily did not survive to see the opening two years later. The building is an ornate one, with a central lofty hall surrounded by a balcony at first-floor level, and exhibition rooms leading off the balcony and central hall. The museum was enlarged in 1974 with an extension of stark simplicity that contrasts sharply with the baroque appearance of the original, but provides modern facilities for the major exhibitions programme and the care and storage of the Glynn Vivian's varied collections.

Over the years the collections have been enriched greatly through the generosity of local benefactors. In 1964, for example, the already extensive collection of Swansea and Nantgarw porcelain was increased through the bequest of Kildare S. Meager of Pennard, Gower. As a result of this gift, the Glynn Vivian now possesses an unrivalled collection of porcelain representing practically every type of ware produced by the renowned Cambrian and Glamorgan factories in the 18th and early 19th centuries. The museum's holdings have also been increased by gifts and grant aid from national bodies, such as the National Art Collections Fund, the Contemporary Art Society, the Contemporary Art Society for Wales, and the Museums and Galleries Commission grant aid scheme, as well as through the support of the Gallery's Association of Friends, established in the 1950s.

Interior view of the entrance hall

The collection of 18th century drinking glasses and of a large assortment of glass paper-weights is impressive, while the John Deffett Francis collection of prints and drawings is an extensive one. The museum has a wide-ranging picture collection, including early Italian works and several from the 18th and 19th centuries. 20th century works are more often on view as they tend to be in better condition. These include paintings by Welsh artists, many of whom have won recognition outside the Principality, for example Evan Walters, Augustus John (colour plate 7) and Gwen John, Morland Lewis, Ceri Richards and Kyffin Williams. There is also a large group of Swansea marine paintings.

The Glynn Vivian, which plays an important part in the life of the city of Swansea and surrounding area, also houses many temporary and constantly changing art exhibitions. Up to thirty a year are staged, showing fine art, craft, photography, design, and large-scale sculpture in the purpose-built outdoor sculpture court. Recent major exhibitions have included 'Turner in Wales', 'Contrariwise' (Surrealism) and 'Sutherland in Wales'. Major financial support is received from the Welsh Arts Council and West Wales Arts. The Gallery also has a Community Arts Officer and runs a full programme of varied activities both within and outside the Gallery. There is a popular Gallery shop selling cards, gifts, prints, books and occasional craft items.

The Curator of the Glynn Vivian is also responsible for the care of the British Empire Panels, painted by Sir Frank Brangwyn and installed in Swansea's beautiful Guildhall, built in 1933. The seventeen panels, rejected by the Royal Fine Arts Commission for the House of Lords, have found a worthy home in Brangwyn Hall, although Swansea's connection with the glory of the British Empire is perhaps a little tenuous. Nevertheless, Frank Brangwyn was of Anglo-Welsh descent. The panels can be seen by making a prior appointment with the Guildhall Superintendent (0792 301301; access is restricted at certain times if concerts or other events are taking place in the Brangwyn Hall). A publication with full colour illustrations of the panels is available from the Glynn Vivian.

Rare early Swansea saltglaze bowl, dated 1778

Drawing of Lyndra *by Augustus John (1878–1961)*

Nantgarw 'carp' plate

Swansea Maritime and Industrial Museum

South Dock, Swansea, West Glamorgan SA1 1SN (0792) 50351/470371
Open daily. F ☕ P ♿ W
🚸 & 👥 preferably book in advance: contact Education Officer.

The old derelict dockland area of Swansea has been completely transformed within the last few years, and the Maritime Quarter, with its marina and leisure facilities, high quality housing and hotels, is a remarkable development within walking distance of the city centre.

Swansea has a long history as an industrial centre, and until comparatively recently the industries of the Swansea area were almost entirely based on metal processing. The smelting of non-ferrous metals such as lead, copper and zinc, the manufacture of iron and steel and the coating of these to make tinplate and other products, gained for Swansea in the 19th century a reputation as the world's metallurgical capital. The city was, and still remains, a very important centre of industry, and it was only right that Swansea should have set about the task of creating a museum to interpret the remarkable story of its industrial development. In 1977 a large warehouse standing on the quayside of the filled-in South Dock, in the middle of industrial decay, was opened as a museum of industry. For years the warehouse stood in isolation amongst the ruins and dereliction, but since those early days the area has been transformed. South Dock was cleared, new lock gates installed, and the old trading dock entered a new era as a centre for maritime leisure. Derelict buildings were improved and given new uses, and the old railway sidings and warehouses made way for stylish quality residences and business premises. The Swansea Maritime and Industrial Museum is in the heart of this new development, and has a vital role to play in the exciting growth of the Maritime Quarter.

The steam tug, 'Canning'

The core of the permanent exhibition at the museum is an exploration of Swansea's past as an industrial centre. This history of the non-ferrous metal industries is presented, as is the history of transport in the area. Swansea was the first town in Wales to have an electric tramway, but it is a great pity that all that remains of the clattering trams that ran from Swansea along the shore of the beautiful bay to the seaside resort of Mumbles is the front end of a double-decker car, which is now displayed in the newly-built tram shed adjacent to the museum in Dylan Thomas Square.

An unusual feature of the Swansea Maritime and Industrial Museum is a complete working woollen mill, installed on the upper floor of the museum building. The Abbey Woollen Mill from the Neath Valley operated in its original setting until the mid-1970s and provided 'check blankets, tweeds, travelling rugs, Welsh shawls, socks, stockings and knitting yarn'. It was a fully comprehensive mill, with all the processes of textile production from sorting raw wool through to carding, spinning, weaving and finishing. The museum was fortunate enough to retain the services of the erstwhile owner of the mill, the redoubtable Mr Griffith Jones, as the manager of the museum's mill until his retirement in 1985. The Jones family, who hailed from North Wales, were well known textile manufacturers, and their traditions of workmanship were transferred to the museum's mill. The products now made have therefore hardly changed in a hundred years, and items produced are obtainable from the museum shop.

Exterior view of the museum, a general goods warehouse of c. 1900

In addition to being an important

Some of the museum's static and marine engines

The Lightship LV 91, the 'Helwick'

centre of manufacture, Swansea was, and still is, an important port, and its history as a cargo and passenger port is explored by means of models and photographs in the museum display. Swansea had been a port from the earliest times, but its first real growth came in the 16th century during the industrial change from charcoal to coal. By 1700 it was common to find as many as a hundred sailing ships waiting to load coal mined from shallow mines, no more than a couple of miles from the sea. With the growth of industrial undertakings, especially the copper industry after the first copper smelter was built in 1717, the port of Swansea really took off. Copper ships from Amlwch and Chile brought ores to Swansea, and the feverish development of docks to cope with the ever-increasing trade was launched from 1850 onwards.

In the South Dock itself, the museum maintains several vessels restored to first class condition. The steam tug 'Canning' was typical of the tug-boats utilised in Swansea docks for the towage of vessels from the open sea to the port, while the 'Helwick lightship' reminds the visitor that navigation and safety in the Bristol Channel was dependent once upon fully-manned light vessels rather than automatically-controlled light buoys. Traffic in the Bristol Channel to Bristol and Cardiff, Newport and Barry, was so extensive that a chain of lightships, as well as shore-located lighthouses, was a prerequisite of safety in the Channel. The vessels are reached from the quayside of the South Dock by a series of walkways that are open daily from April to September.

Swansea was more than a trading port that accommodated cargo vessels from all quarters of the globe: it was also a fishing port of considerable importance. In Swansea Bay there was a large oyster fishery, while set-netting for a variety of flatfish was widely practised in the area. Towards the end of the 19th century, with the widespread adoption of steam for the propulsion of ships, Swansea attained considerable importance as a centre of deep-sea fishing. One such vessel, the 'Katie Ann', a beam trawler that operated out of Swansea, has been preserved by the museum and forms a very important part of the attractions in the South Dock.

Interior of the Abbey Woollen Mill

The Swansea Museum (Royal Institution of South Wales)

Victoria Road, Swansea, West Glamorgan SA1 1SN (0792) 653763

Closed Sundays and Mondays. £ P
♿ S: no access for wheelchairs, except with manual assistance.
welcome.
book in advance: contact Education Officer.
Access to the collections for study, by appointment, is welcomed: apply to The Administrator.

Drawing for the print of 'An East View of Swansea' published 1748 (detail)

Early photograph of a cottage at Parkmill, Gower, nr Swansea, c. 1860

The Swansea Museum, in the centre of the commercial heart of this most prosperous of Welsh ports, is Wales' oldest public museum. It concentrates on locally-based historical and general interest displays, with reference to the area around Swansea. These complement the displays on other aspects at the nearby **Swansea Industrial and Maritime Museum** and at the **Glynn Vivian Art Gallery and Museum**. Unlike these municipal undertakings, however, the Swansea Museum is operated by a voluntary society, The Royal Institution of South Wales, founded in 1834. The museum was built in 1835 to house the Institution's growing collections, and is an elegant Grade II listed building, with Bath-stone classical frontage and Ionic portico that are a prominent feature of the southern entrance to Swansea. In 1973 a formal partnership agreement with the University College, Swansea, appeared to secure the future of the museum, but subsequent financial pressures on universities resulted in the ending of this arrangement in 1986. Despite limited public funding since, the future is very uncertain. In the meantime, the museum continues to provide a good overall introduction to the locality and an essential research facility.

Most of the displays are descriptive of west Glamorgan, particularly Swansea and the Gower peninsula. This area lies on the coal-measures and the origins of these are explained in the geology gallery. The archaeology gallery shows items from local excavations, with explanations of their contexts. The past is covered in sequence, commencing with the prehistoric Gower caves and continuing via Iron-Age and Roman fortifications to post-medieval pottery, found with the original kiln. The china gallery shows what must be the finest display – in extent and in quality – of the products of the noted Swansea potteries (late 18th to early 19th centuries) from both the Cambrian Pottery (including its 'Swansea China') and the rather later Glamorgan Pottery.

The natural history gallery has modern environmental settings emphasising habitats, together with more traditional (and older) collections of butterflies and other insects.

The museum has a very large collection of original drawings and watercolours, the majority of which illustrate the topography of the town over the last 200 years, which has seen tremendous changes. Swansea was one of the centres of pioneer photography and there is a large collection of local photographs, with many of the earliest dating from the 1840s. A selection of these and of the early watercolours is on public display. The whole of these and other reserve collections are accessible for research, by arrangement. Researchers may similarly use the extensive collections of manuscripts and rare printed books, as well as other sources, which are directly relevant to local historical research. The museum's archives include, for example, a complete run of *The Cambrian*, the Swansea newspaper founded in 1804.

Transfer-printed earthenware dish, Cambrian Pottery, Swansea, c. 1848

Swansea pottery tea jar, 1778

Golden Eagle

Satirical print of the Duke of Beaufort's steward in Wind Street, Swansea, 1787 (detail)

Although not of directly local interest, there is a small display of early Egyptian items, including the mummy of a priest of Isis. This is a great favourite with younger visitors.

The displays and collections of the Swansea Museum are of interest to the general public and to serious students alike. Let us hope this historic museum can continue to survive the pressures of these hard financial times.

TENBY

Tenby Museum

Castle Hill, Tenby, Pembrokeshire, Dyfed SA70 7BP (0834) 2809
Open daily Easter to October, late evening opening July and August; restricted opening November to Easter. £
♿ S: wheelchair access difficult.
🚻 & 👥 must book in advance; pre-booked 👥 F.

The beautiful seaside town of Tenby, although best known as a holiday resort, was the site of an ancient settlement, first mentioned in a poem in the 9th century. It is a walled town with its own character and personality, for with the arrival of the Normans in the late 11th century the value of Tenby as a fine natural fortress, which could be supplied from the sea at times of siege, was quickly realised. The town grew very rapidly and in the middle ages became the most important port in south Pembrokeshire, importing French wine and other foreign goods, and exporting locally-mined anthracite. It was granted its Mayoral charter in 1402, and by Tudor times was one of the most important ports of west Wales, when its trade was dominated by a class of rich merchant burgesses, evidence of whose solid stone houses can still be seen in the old town.

The history of the borough is displayed in the Tenby Museum, and the charters that survive together with the ceremonial maces (which are still used on civic occasions and date from the reign of Charles I) may be seen in the Entrance Hall. As a fishing and trading port, it was of great importance, and that aspect of history is well described in a new maritime gallery; for Tenby was, according to Defoe, 'a very good road for shipping and well frequented . . . a good fishery for herring in its season, a great colliery, or rather export of coals and they give a very considerable trade to Ireland'. In the gallery are exhibited models and drawings of the unique Tenby sailing lugger, used by generations of fishermen for the capture of herring and other fish, while appropriately the Tenby lifeboat, which is still launched from a slipway near the museum, is well represented in the exhibition.

By the late 18th century, the trading activities of the port of Tenby had declined considerably, and it was around this time that Tenby began to assume its new role as a fashionable watering place and seaside resort. Although it remained an important fishing base throughout the 19th century, the period witnessed the emergence of Tenby as a typical Victorian seaside town, complete with bathing machines, a bandstand, hotels, boarding houses and a pier. The arrival of the railway in 1863 accelerated Tenby's development as a resort, making it easier for tourists to reach the town from all parts of the country. Thus, while its trade withered away, Tenby became the mecca for countless day trips and Sunday school expeditions from the South Wales valleys.

In the Victorian era, a museum inevitably became an essential amenity for a town geared to tourism. A number of local people decided to set up a museum in 1878, in what was once a school within the precincts of the cas-

The South Beach, Tenby, in the 1890s

tle; the building is still occupied by the Tenby Museum. The original function of the museum was to house a collection of archaeological material assembled by the Rev. G.N. Smith, Rector of Gumfreston, from his excavations in local caves in the Tenby area and on nearby Caldey Island. Throughout its existence, the museum has been administered on behalf of the town by a local committee with honorary curators and officers, and has been fortunate in attracting particularly able and dedicated individuals. The name of one of those eminent curators is preserved in the excellent Wilfred Harrison Picture Gallery.

The museum has a large collection of paintings, engravings and drawings, many of them depicting scenes of the Tenby area and including work by such artists as Ibbetson and Gastineau. Tenby was the birthplace of Augustus John (1878–1961) and Nina Hamnett (1890–1956). Charles Norris (1799–1856) lived and painted in Tenby from 1805 until his death.

The geology and archaeology of Pembrokeshire are interpreted in an outstanding new gallery; another displays the animal and bird life of the area and coastline.

One unusual exhibition is that relating to the last invasion of Britain, when in February 1797 a force of 1500 men landed on Carreg Wastad near Fishguard. The exploits of the Castlemartin troop of the Pembrokeshire Yeomanry, who were involved with the defeat of the rag bag of invading French soldiers and convicts, is shown in an interesting display. The uniforms and weapons of the Yeomanry are also noteworthy.

Of course, a substantial part of what is really a general museum, concerned with interpreting all aspects of life in the Tenby region, is devoted to the development of Tenby as a seaside resort. Interest in the health-inducing properties of seawater and the birth of coastal spas came about in the mid-18th century and, in spite of its remoteness from centres of population, Tenby was soon discovered by those with the time and the stamina to withstand the journey by coach or sea. The houses, baths, assembly rooms and theatre necessary to accommodate visitors and cater for their interests were soon constructed. Early major developments were financed by Sir William Paxton, who first appeared on the Tenby scene in 1805.

Julius Caesar Ibbetson, A Dragnet at Tenby

Part of the Archaeology gallery

Model of a Tenby Lugger

Tenby's location ensured that it remained fairly exclusive until late in the 19th century, and its wealth of marine life attracted biologists, whose enthusiasm captured the interest of other visitors. The coming of the railway extended, if only gradually, the range of residential visitors, and brought excursionists from the industrial towns for a day at the sea. The increased demand for accommodation took the town beyond its medieval walls into the South Cliff area fronted by the Esplanade. Its spectacular scenery and superb beaches have combined to make Tenby an ideal family resort. But even with improved communications, its geographical position has preserved Tenby from over-development into a fun-fair resort. The history of those years is outlined in a book, 'Fair and Fashionable Tenby', which accompanies the exhibition. The displays in the Lobby, the Picture Gallery and the Local History Gallery upstairs evoke Tenby's colourful past, and add to an enjoyment of the town of today.

TREHAFOD

Rhondda Heritage Park

Lewis Merthyr, Coed Cae Road, Trehafod, Mid Glamorgan CF37 7NP (0443) 682036
Visitor Centre open Wednesdays to Sundays (may be extended in summer – check in advance). £ ♿ W

The Rhondda Heritage Park is a museum in the making, and it will take many years to fulfil the ambitious plans that have been drawn up by three local authorities and two statutory bodies. It has the aim of becoming the premier heritage attraction for South Wales, but the fulfillment of this dream depends very heavily on the availability of financial resources. Undoubtedly, the Rhondda Valleys and their overwhelming dependence on the coal industry deserve interpretation, for the Rhondda is probably the most famous and evocative of all British industrial regions. The function of the Heritage Park will be the presentation, in the most concise and inspiring way, of something of the character, personality and spirit of the Rhondda. A Visitor Centre, opened in summer 1989, provides an introduction to the overall development of the Park and its themes.

Winding gear and colliery buildings

In 1983 the closure of the Lewis–Merthyr/Tŷ Mawr collieries signalled the disappearance of all coal mines in the area, and the Heritage Park will provide a major tourist and recreational project that will form a focus for, and a gateway to, the Rhondda and South Wales valleys. Progress has been made on the regeneration of a desperately derelict site, and there are ambitious plans for the presentation of a number of themes associated with the life of the people of the Rhondda. The authorities have certainly kept clear of the term 'museum', but as far as the history of the people is concerned existing buildings and structures will be utilised to present the story.

The first theme to be explored will be the Story of Coal, the industry that was until recent times the life-blood of

General view of the Rhondda Heritage Park site (the bridge has since been demolished)

the community. This section will focus on the winding gear and associated colliery buildings at the Lewis Merthyr and nearby Tŷ Mawr Collieries. These buildings and the machinery they contain are being restored and interpreted. A particular aspect of the mining exhibition will be the emphasis placed on the human story associated with the extraction of coal in the valleys over the course of a century and a half. The display will include an underground feature, but a far more relevant aspect explored will be the community life and its hardships, the community spirit, and the famous people that came from the Rhondda.

The second theme to be explored will be the choral and musical traditions of the Rhondda, which will form an important element in the programme of events for the site. Initially, events will be staged in the refurbished pit-head baths, but in due course a purpose-built auditorium and practice rooms will house this thematic enterprise. It will be developed over a number of years to provide a choral centre that will be a home for choir practices and year-round performances.

There are also plans to recreate a mining village, to build an events arena, and to landscape the site. The project is indeed a very ambitious one, that if successful could be a major attraction; but there is always a danger of the site deteriorating into a fun palace. 'There might be a recreated cinema actually showing period films complete with organist; ice cream and fish and chips wrapped in a reproduction period newspaper might be sold from a period tricycle and shop respectively; perhaps visitors might even be given period money to use at period prices; their allowances being equal to a miner's pay packet', so the initial report on the project stated. One is perhaps a little apprehensive of the eventual outcome of the scheme, for it is another example of solving serious economic distress by providing a tourist facility. Proximity to the M4 has seemed to be a far more important consideration than the provision of an interpretative facility that the Rhondda deserves.

USK

Gwent Rural Life Museum

The Malt Barn, New Market Street, Usk, Gwent NP5 1AU (02913) 3777

Open daily April to September (except weekend mornings), otherwise by appointment. £ P

♿ S: wheelchair access to ground floor and yard only.

🚻 & 👥 book in advance, admission possible all year, anytime, by arrangement: contact Museum or Hon. Sec. Mrs S.M. Williams, 14 St Cybi Avenue, Llangybi, Usk, tel (Tredunnock) 315.

This museum, manned entirely by voluntary labour, is run by the Rural Crafts Preservation Society. The museum was established in 1966 in Llanfapley, near Abergavenny, but soon outgrew that space, and in 1981 was moved to the attractive market town of Usk, to a building owned by the Monmouth District Council. The Malt Barn in which the museum is now housed is a fascinating building, and probably served as a barn for the adjacent maltster's house. The craft of malting barley for domestic and commercial beer brewing was of considerable importance in such an area as rural Gwent, and the remains of many malting houses may still be found in the area. The earliest known record of the Usk Malt Barn is a lease of 1791, but much of the structure appears older. With the addition of a Victorian cottage at the back of the Barn, the museum building has a very attractive appearance.

Part of the Harvesting display

Various traps

The main purpose of the museum is to depict the rural life of Gwent over a period of about two centuries. Agriculture was, of course, the mainstay of the economy of the region, and a substantial section of the exhibition space is devoted to the activities of the farm. The four seasons of the countryman's year are displayed through the tools and implements used in various seasonal tasks, but the most important items in the museum's collections are the four-wheeled farm wagons. The one painted in Venetian red is a typical Monmouth box wagon, heavy and sturdy, used for a variety of tasks around

The museum's Monmouth Box Wagon

the farm. It carried the hay, corn and root crop harvest; apples from the orchards to the cider mills; and was used for carrying some heavy loads, such as gravel and building stones. The other wagon on display is a much more delicate vehicle altogether: this is the traditional Glamorgan harvest bow wagon, painted blue, which carried the chattels of a local farming family to Gwent in the early 1900s. The Glamorgan wagon, probably the most beautiful and graceful of all the regional types of four-wheeled farm vehicles, is very rare, and no more than four have been preserved in museum collections.

The display of craft tools at the Gwent Rural Life Museum is extensive, but most represent those vital crafts, such as carpentry and blacksmithing, that were essential in every rural community. In country districts in the past, most of the countryman's help could be supplied from within each community, and the craftsmen that fulfilled the needs for tools of agriculture, and furnishings and equipment of the home and dairy, were numerous. But in addition to the equipment used by professional craftsmen of the area, the museum also contains an extensive collection of equipment used in the home. Buttermaking and barrel-making figure prominently in the collections, while a complete cider mill awaits restoration and display. Of course, rural Gwent was an important cider-making region, and the apple orchards attached to almost every farm produced vast quantities of apples that were pressed in many cider houses throughout the area.

The Victorian cottage attached to the main building of the museum contains items relating to the domestic pursuits of Gwent. Laundry equipment and cooking utensils, hearth furniture and smocks are found in the cottage, and a tray in Pontypool japanned ware reminds us that the market town of Usk at one time had a japanned-ware factory.

The Gwent Rural Life Museum is an excellent example of an important collection that came into being through the enthusiasm and energy of local people. Its methods of display may lack the sophistication of wealthier, professionally manned establishments, but the authenticity of its well-documented collection of rural artefacts is something that can be admired. That excellence was recognised in 1983, when the museum won a Prince of Wales award for its work in preserving the heritage of the rural life of the area.

WELSHPOOL

Powysland Museum and Montgomery Canal Centre

The Canal Wharf, Welshpool, Powys SY21 7AQ (0938) 554633 (Powysland Museum located at Salop Road, Welshpool, Powys SY21 7EG until Easter 1990).

Closed lunchtimes, Saturday mornings and all day Sundays; closed Wednesdays in winter. F ♿ 🚻 & 🚻 book in advance with Curator if talk or handling sessions are required.

The Powysland Club is amongst the oldest local history societies in Britain. Formed in 1867 by a group of historians living in and around the important market town of Welshpool, the aim of the Powysland Club was to promote interest in and record all aspects of the history of the region. The Club still flourishes today, holding regular meetings and publishing its very high quality journal – *The Montgomeryshire Collections*. At the early meetings of the Powysland Club, members exhibited their own personal collections, and in 1874 a new building to accommodate the club and its collections was built in Salop Road; it also accommodates a first-class library. Typical of purpose-built Victorian museum buildings, it has the badge of the Powysland Club on its yellow brick frontage. To mark Queen Victoria's Jubilee in 1887 the private museum was transferred under trust to the town, but in 1974 it became the responsibility of the Powys County Council.

Tools of the white cooper, who made dairy and household utensils

Agricultural exhibits

At the time of writing, the museum collections are in the process of being moved from the building in Salop Road to a more centrally located site – an old, restored warehouse beside the Montgomery Canal. A Grade II listed building, the canal-side warehouse is also near the railway station. The Powysland Museum and Montgomery Canal Centre is scheduled to open at Easter 1990.

In recent years the Powysland Museum has collected material that is of relevance to the life and history of the eastern section of the old county of Montgomery, stretching as far as the English border. This limitation of the collection was never imposed in the early days of the museum, for much of the material collected related to foreign countries, especially to material emanating from the outposts to the British Empire. That ethnographic material is still on display but is dedicated to the founders of the museum, many of whom were distinguished members of the colonial service.

The new displays will give an introduction to the history of Welshpool and Montgomeryshire, using the varied material that a local history museum typically collects. Dairy and domestic utensils, and an extensive collection of artefacts relating to agriculture, reflect the main occupation of the inhabitants of eastern Montgomery. One gallery in the new museum will illustrate the agricultural and industrial development of the area, including the important role played by both railway and canal. The local crafts, typical of a rural community that was dependent on its own resources for all means of life, form a substantial part of the collection on display. There are the ordinary tools of boot-mending, hat-making and carpentry, but there is also an unusual collection of the tools of a white cooper, who until 1962 practised his trade in a workshop located directly opposite the museum in Salop Road. The white cooper made pails, butter churns, washtubs and other utensils for dairy and household use. The Welshpool white cooper was almost certainly the last to practice his trade in Wales.

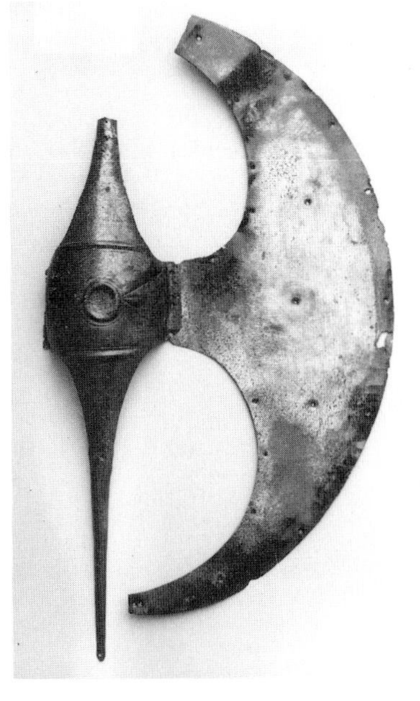

The Moel Hirradug shield

Archaeological work in the region is in the care of the Clwyd-Powys Archaeological Trust, and recent archaeological items acquired by the museum are principally those presented by the Trust. The early members of the Powysland Club were able and enthusiastic excavators, and many objects from their work are on display. A Bronze Age beaker, the Moel Hirradug Iron Age shield, and finds from a Roman burial site in Welshpool are all of national importance. An archaeological gallery in the new museum will focus on finds in Montgomeryshire and the work of the Trust.

The museum's Bronze Age beaker

WREXHAM

Bersham Industrial Heritage Centre

Bersham, Wrexham, Clwyd
LL14 4HT (0978) 261529
Closed lunchtimes and all day Mondays (except Bank Holidays); also closed Sunday mornings Easter to October and otherwise all day Sunday. F P ♿
🚻 & 👥 book in advance if a guide required.

The interpretative centre at Bersham, relating to the industrial development of an important manufacturing district on the western outskirts of Wrexham, is really the starting point for an industrial history trail that is eight miles in length. From *Erddig*, one of the National Trust's most fascinating houses, to the lead-mining village of Minera, the area has much to offer to those interested in industrial history.

Much of the exhibition at the interpretative centre, which occupies an old Victorian school in the centre of the village of Bersham, is concerned with the history of iron-making in the area. The ironworks at Bersham was founded by Charles Lloyd in 1718, although it did not reach its peak until the 1780s when John Wilkinson expanded the works. Lloyd was a friend of Abraham Darby of Coalbrookdale, and provided some of the funding for Darby's first experiment with coke for smelting iron at Coalbrookdale in 1709. This eventually led to the successful smelting of iron with coke at Bersham in 1721. From 1727 Abraham Darby's son-in-law operated the Bersham Furnace. The real development of the industrial village took place with the arrival of the Wilkinson family in 1753, and in 1762 the famous pioneer of the iron industry, John 'Iron Mad' Wilkinson, was producing cannons and cylinders, as well as a wide range of other items including pipes, shells, grenades, guns and box heaters. He later extended the

Exterior view of Bersham Industrial Heritage Centre

John Wilkinson

works, and was responsible for boring the cylinders for James Watt's famous steam engine of 1775 (he continued to make cylinders for Watt's engines for the next twenty years). Indeed, so important was the Bersham works in the 1770s that James Watt sent his eldest son to study at Bersham.

The period up to the 1790s was particularly prosperous for the Wilkinson family. Bersham produced large numbers of cannon during the American War of Independence (1775–83) in addition to steam engines, which came to the fore again after. John Wilkinson purchased the impressive Brymbo Hall estate in 1793. But by then relations with his brother and partner, William, had deteriorated (between 1777 and 1785 William had been employed in France, erecting two state ironworks, and the brothers had fallen out on his return). Their quarrel led to the decline of Bersham Works and by the end of 1795 they were sold. John revived a smaller works during the next few years, but Bersham never recovered. After his death in 1808 the work's continued in operation under his nephew, but were sold by auction in 1812, after which a paper mill was built on the rolling mill meadow and part of the site converted to a corn mill.

There are still a number of buildings in the area that bear witness to its prosperity as one of the foremost manufacturing regions of Wales. A weir across the river Clywedog probably provided power originally for the furnaces, and later for Wilkinson's cannon boring mill; after the works closed it powered the corn mill. Part of a row of cottages that once housed iron workers is still in place, while the Accounts House for the Bersham ironworks dominates the centre of the village. The most striking of all the buildings is an octagonal one that was almost certainly a cannon foundry, while nearby is Bersham Mill, originally built as a foundry and later adapted to a corn mill. Newly-constructed cannons were tested for accuracy by firing

The Bersham Mill building, with the Accounts House in the background

Blacksmith at the museum's forge

shots at a ballistics bank, remains of which can still be seen. Most of the cannon made was used in the American War of Independence, but it is said that a large proportion of the cannons used by the British army in the Peninsular War, as well as those used in the Russian and Turkish wars, were also made at Bersham.

John Wilkinson (1728–1808) was certainly a pioneer of the iron industry. The boring mill that he patented, initially used for guns, was adapted soon afterwards for steam-engine cylinders, and Wilkinson made a major contribution to the efficiency of the steam engine. The Bersham Industrial Heritage Centre and the Industrial Trail are a tribute to this pioneer.

Another family of iron workers represented at the Bersham Industrial Heritage Centre, perhaps less well known than the Wilkinsons, is that of the Davies Brothers, gatemakers extraordinary. At Croes Foel smithy near Bersham, the brothers aroused considerable fame as wrought-iron smiths, their best-known work being the gates to Chirk Castle. A focal point of the Davies brothers' exhibition at the Centre is the authentically reconstructed forge, complete with anvil, bellows and tools.

Wrexham Maelor Heritage Centre

47–49 King Street, Wrexham, Clwyd LL11 1HR (0978) 290048
Closed Thursday mornings and all day Sundays. F P ♿
🚻 & 👥 book in advance.

Wrexham, the largest town in North Wales, does not yet possess its own museum, although there are plans to establish a full-scale museum service in the foreseeable future. The Council employs a full-time curator and museum registrar, has an active collecting policy, and a number of books and pamphlets explaining all aspects of the natural and cultural heritage of this fascinating part of Wales have been produced. Additionally, impressive exhibitions explaining the local environment are organised on a regular basis at the Wrexham Library Arts Centre. In 1987 a new Heritage Centre was opened, which is seen as the Wrexham Maelor Council's first phase of its Museum Development Plan. A large number of exhibits have been collected, documented and conserved, and the Council now possesses the nucleus of a good collection of local material, much of which is on display at the Heritage Centre.

One of the most fascinating, but perhaps the least well-known of the activities of the Wrexham Maelor district until recent times was the brick, tile and terrocotta industry, which is well represented in the museum's collections. It is an industry that goes back for many centuries, for the glacial and alluvial clays of the area were used in Roman times for the production of bricks, tiles and other items of pottery. With the departure of the Romans, the industry declined, but in the 17th century it was revived. In the 18th and 19th centuries the industry flourished tremendously, and the town of Ruabon where the industry was centred was known as 'Terracottopolis'. The pro-

Ruby lustre tile made c. 1890

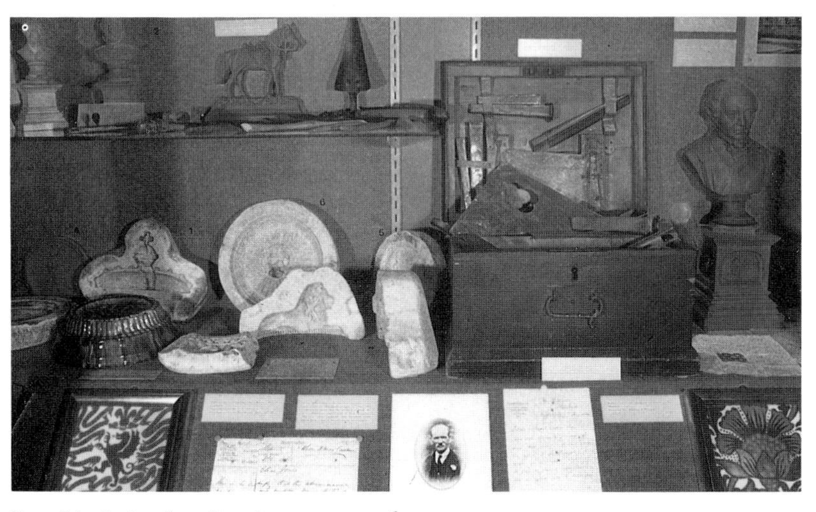

Part of the display about tile and terracotta manufacture

Painted dial from a longcase clock by Thomas Heywood of Wrexham, c. 1860

First World War display

ducts of the industry were exported in great quantities, and those of local makers, such as the factories of Monk and Newell, J.C. Edwards, and Dennis, were widely utilised in the rapidly expanding urban conglomerations of the 19th century. The Victoria Law Courts built in Brimingham in 1887–91 were faced with terracotta tiles produced by J.C. Edwards of Ruabon, while the products of the brick and terracotta works of Ruabon provided the Wrexham area with its red-brick appearance.

Wrexham, as an early market town, had its share of craft industries, which supplied the needs of an extensive agricultural and industrial hinterland. Here the printing and brewing industries flourished, and Wrexham Lager is still produced for an extensive market. The museum possesses a substantial collection of coopers' tools, for that intricate and highly skilled craft was an essential activity in breweries.

One particular trade associated with the district was that of watch and clock manufacture, and an important collection of long-case clocks by local clockmakers is found in the museum. The importance of Wrexham as the centre of the now almost defunct North Wales coalfield is represented by a collection of documents, artefacts and photographs relating to that industry.

Wrexham, often described as 'the Capital of North Wales', has much to offer; it is a businesslike workaday town, which is a natural hub for an extensive area. Its parish church, which is said to have been the inspiration for the Victorian tower of the Houses of Parliament, is regarded as one of the 'Seven Wonders of Wales', and the borough's ambitious plans for a proper museum, when they come to fruition, will dispel the image of Clwyd as 'the Cinderella of Welsh Counties as far as museums are concerned'.

Other Museums in Wales

Please note that many of the museums listed below are *only open in summer*; check with museums for opening times. Some are *open only by appointment.*

ABERDYFI

Outward Bound Sailing Museum
The Wharf, Aberdyfi, Gwynedd
(0654) 72464

Associated with the Outward Bound School located in this once-important port; displays illustrate the history of sailing and sailing ships in the area.

ABERGAVENNY

Abergavenny Museum
The Castle, Castle Street, Abergavenny, Gwent
NP7 5EE (0873) 4282

A local authority museum concerned mainly with the history of the market town, its castle, dating from the 12th–14th century, rural crafts and the obligatory 'ye olde Welsh kitchen'.

ABERGYNOLWYN

Abergynolwyn Village Museum
Y Gorlan, 17 Water Street, Abergynolwyn, Tywyn, Gwynedd LL36 9YB

A small, locally run museum devoted to the history of an important slate-quarrying village.

ABERYSTWYTH

Aberystwyth Yesterday
The Little Chapel, New Street, Aberystwyth, Dyfed
(0970) 617119

A private collection of prints, photographs and artefacts relating to the history of this seaside town. A part of the collection is housed in the Railway Station buildings.

Aberystwyth College Collection
Penglais, Aberystwyth, Dyfed
SY23 3BU (0970) 3339

Prints, drawings and ceramics.

BARMOUTH

Barmouth Lifeboat Museum
R.N.L.I. Museum, Pen-y-cei, The Harbour, Barmouth, Gwynedd LL42 1EH.

A small museum devoted to the history of the lifeboat service in this once important port.

Tŷ Crwn
Barmouth, Gwynedd
(0341) 422341 ext. 263

A medieval tower house containing material obtained from the *Bronze Bell* shipwreck of the 15th century.

BEDDGELERT

Sygun Copper Mine
Beddgelert, Gwynedd
(076686) 595

A restored copper mine that sets out to interpret the history of copper mining in North Wales.

BETWS-Y-COED

Conwy Valley Railway Museum
The Old Goods Yard, Betws-y-Coed, Gwynedd LL24 0AL
(06902) 568

Narrow gauge and standard gauge railway items displayed in railway buildings in a village that is amongst the most frequented tourist traps in North Wales. Includes an operating model railway and steam-hauled miniature railway.

BLAENAU FFESTINIOG

Gloddfa Ganol Slate Mine
Blaenau Ffestiniog, Gwynedd
(0766) 830664

The world's largest slate mine; contains Mining, Railway and Wildlife Museums in the surface workings.

Llechwedd Slate Caverns
Blaenau Ffestiniog, Gwynedd
LL41 3NB (0766) 830306

An interpretation of the town's most important activity in an impressive slate mining complex, complete with underground tours.

Moelwyn Mill
Tanygrisiau, Blaenau Ffestiniog, Gwynedd

A restored water-driven woollen mill that contains one of the few examples of fulling stocks preserved in Britain.

BRECON

The South Wales Borderers (24th Foot) & The Monmouthshire Regiment Museum
The Barracks, The Watton, Brecon, Powys LD3 7EB
(0874) 3111 ext. 2310

Museum of the South Wales Borderers & Monmouthshire Regiment, now part of the Royal Regiment of Wales (24th/41st foot). Contains a special Zulu Wars exhibition.

CAERNARFON

Segontium Roman Fort Museum
Beddgelert Road, Caernarfon, Gwynedd (0286) 5625

Tells the story of the conquest and occupation of Wales by the Romans. Also displays finds from the excavations at *Segontium*, the famous Roman auxiliary fort overlooking Caernarfon.

CALDICOT

Caldicot Castle Museum
The Castle, Caldicot, Gwent
NP6 4HU (0291) 420241

Restored Norman Castle with a small local history museum and art gallery with regular exhibitions.

CARDIFF

Cardiff Castle
Cardiff, South Glamorgan
CF1 2RB (0222) 822084

The impressive Burges-designed castle in the city centre houses a collection of material relating to the civic affairs of the capital. The Castle itself is fully furnished.

Museum of the First Queen's Dragoon Guards
Cardiff Castle, Cardiff, South Glamorgan (0222) 27611

Regimental museum.

CARDIGAN

Geler Jones Museum
North Road, Cardigan, Dyfed
(0239) 612573

A very large private, miscellaneous collection of farm implements, tools, household items and craft equipment; *open by arrangement* with the owners.

CORRIS

Corris Railway Museum
Station Yard, Corris, Machynlleth, Powys
SY20 9SS (065473) 343

Devoted to the story of a narrow gauge railway that operated from 1890 to 1948. Occupies an old railway building in the centre of the slate village of Corris.

CYNWYL ELFED

Y Gangell
Blaenycoed, Cynwyl Elfed, Dyfed (09948) 220

A museum devoted to Wales' well known poet and hymnologist, the Revd H. Elfed Lewis. *Open by appointment only.*

GLYNARTHEN

Pen-bont-bren Farm Museum
Glynarthen, Dyfed (0239) 810248

A miscellaneous collection of farm and domestic equipment, which forms a part of the Pen-bont-bren Farm Hotel.

GLYN CEIRIOG

Chwarel Wynne Mine and Museum
Glyn Ceiriog, nr Llangollen, Clwyd (069172) 345

A slate quarry covering a 12-acre site with a small museum included.

Neuadd Goffa Memorial Institute
High Street, Glyn Ceiriog, nr Llangollen, Clwyd (069172) 296

A village hall that contains a small local museum.

HOLYHEAD

Holyhead Maritime Museum
Rhos-y-gaer Avenue, Holyhead, Gwynedd (0407) 2816

Established in 1986 to trace the history of one of the most important of British ferry ports; its display has sections on shipwrecks, marine craftsmen and the whaling industry.

KNIGHTON

Offa's Dyke Centre
Knighton, Powys

An interpretative exhibition in an old school relating to the history and the scenery along the dyke that separated Wales from England.

LAMPETER

Cellan Model Aircraft Museum
Cellan, Nr Lampeter, Dyfed
(0570) 422604

A private collection housed in adapted farm buildings, tracing the history of the RAF and its aircraft since 1920.

LAUGHARNE

Dylan Thomas Boathouse
Cliff Walk, Laugharne, Dyfed
(0267) 234566 ext. 221

A furnished house, once the poet's home, with interpretative panels and audio-visual presentation, all devoted to the memory of the Anglo-Welsh poet.

LLANBERIS

Quarry Hospital
Padarn Country Park, Llanberis, Gwynedd

Refurbished Dinorwic Quarry Hospital on shores of Lake Padarn.

LLANDDEWI

Gower Farm Museum
Luke Farm, Llanddewi, Gower, Nr Swansea, West Glamorgan
(044120) 391195

An exhibition of farm equipment and animals attached to a working homestead.

LLANDUDNO

Llandudno Doll Museum and Model Railway
Masonic Street, Llandudno, Gwynedd LL30 2DU
(0492) 76312

An attraction in North Wales' most important seaside resort.

LLANELLI

Llanelli Public Library and Exhibition Gallery
Vaughan Street, Llanelli, Dyfed
(0554) 773538

A small exhibition gallery mainly for temporary exhibitions.

Trostre Tinplate Works
Llanelli, Dyfed (0554) 741111

A small museum in an old farmhouse adjacent to the modern Trostre Works. *Open by arrangement* with Works Manager.

LLANGERNYW

Sir Henry Jones Cottage Museum
Nanhoron, Plas Aelas, Llangernyw, Clwyd LL22 8BJ

A small social history museum.

LLANGOLLEN

Llangollen Motor Museum
Pentrefelin, Llangollen, Clwyd LL20 8EE 0978 860324

A small museum founded in 1980, with restricted opening hours.

Llangollen Railway Society Ltd
The Station, Abbey Road, Llangollen, Clwyd (0978) 860957

Preserved railway and running stock; trains run in summer season.

MAESLLYN

Maesllyn Woollen Mill Museum
Maesllyn, Nr Llandysul, Dyfed (023975) 251

A museum partly devoted to the textile industry and located in an old mill building. It also has a miscellaneous collection of old radios and television sets, together with a shop and nature trail.

MARGAM

Margam Abbey and Stones Museum
Country Park, Margam, Nr Port Talbot, West Glamorgan (0656) 742618

A museum of Roman, Early Christian and Medieval monumental stones and an interpretative exhibition about the estate, in 800 acres of open parkland used for leisure activities, with a herd of wandering deer.

MATHRY

Llangloffan Farm
Castle Morris, Mathry, Dyfed (03485) 241

A working cheese-making farm with a small museum of dairy utensils.

MERTHYR TUDFUL

Joseph Parry Museum
4 Chapel Row, Merthyr Tudful, Mid Glamorgan DF48 1BN

A terraced house devoted to the memory of the composer Joseph Parry, who was born there although he spent most of his life in Aberystwyth and the USA.

MOLD

Daniel Owen Museum
Earl Road, Mold, Clwyd CH7 1AP (0352) 4791

A museum devoted to Wales' most important 19th century novelist.

MONMOUTH

Royal Monmouthshire Royal Engineers (Militia) Museum
Great Castle House, Monmouth, Gwent (0600) 2935

Regimental museum.

NARBERTH

Blackpool Mill
Canaston Bridge, Narberth, Dyfed SA67 8BL (0834) 813697

A water-driven flour mill containing a country wheel-wright's shop and dubious life-size replicas of the Welsh dragon and prehistoric animals.

NEATH

Neath Museum
Mechanics Institution, 4 Church Place, Neath, West Glamorgan (0639) 65741

A small but developing museum devoted to the history of this industrial town.

NEFYN

Llŷn Historical and Maritime Museum
Old St Mary's Church, Church Street, Nefyn, Gwynedd (0758) 720308

Displays on the life and activities of the local community from the 19th century to the present day with an emphasis on the importance of fishing and seafaring in the life of Nefyn.

NEWCASTLE EMLYN

Felin Geri
Cwmcou, Newcastle Emlyn, Dyfed (0239) 710810

A restored working corn mill and saw mill with all the trappings of a tourist attraction, from a bakery to a rural life museum, wildlife museum and even a Japanese Restaurant.

NEWPORT

Castell Henllys Iron Age Fort
Felindre Farchog, Newport, Dyfed (062) 8824793

Living history, open-air museum with reconstructions, fortifications and craft activity.

NEWTOWN

Robert Owen Museum
Davies Memorial Gallery, The Park, Newtown, Powys SY16 2NZ (0686) 26220

Devoted to the history of the founder of the cooperative movement, who spent the first four years of his life in this once-important industrial town.

PEMBROKE

Castle Hill Museum
Pembroke, Dyfed

A museum of local artefacts established in 1986.

PENMACHNO

Woollen Mill and Museum
Penmachno, Gwynedd (0766) 2785

A museum associated with a working woollen mill and extensive craft retail shop.

PORTHCAWL

Porthcawl Museum
Old Police Station, John Street, Porthcawl, Mid Glamorgan (065) 6713029

A modest museum devoted to the study of this once-important coal exporting port, now a seaside resort.

PORTHMADOG

Ffestiniog Railway Museum
Harbour Station, Porthmadog, Gwynedd LL49 9NF (0766) 2340

Traces the history of the important narrow gauge railway that brought the slates of Blaenau Ffestiniog to its principal exporting port.

Tŷ'n Llan Farm Museum
Porthmadog, Gwynedd

A collection of farm tools and domestic and dairy utensils housed in a farm heavily involved in tourist activities.

PORTMEIRION

Portmeirion Museum
Portmeirion, Nr Penrhyndeudraeth, Gwynedd

A small exhibition area tracing the history of the architecturally unique 'Italian village' designed by Clough Williams-Ellis.

PUMSAINT

Dolau Cothi Gold Mines
Pumsaint, Dyfed (05585) 605

Preserved gold mine with visitor centre and underground visits.

RHAEADR

Rhaeadr Museum
Rhaeadr, Powys

Established in 1986 as a small interpretative exhibition tracing the history of this modest market town.

RHOOSE

Wales Aircraft Museum
Cardiff Airport, Rhoose, Nr Barry, South Glamorgan (0222) 562780

The only aviation museum in the Principality, but does not at present collect or interpret items relating to the development of Welsh aviation, or the important role that Wales played in aviation history.

RISCA

Risca Industrial Archaeological Society Museum
Pontymister Annexe, Risca, Gwent (0633) 612245

A miscellaneous collection of artefacts including the contents of a Cardiff chemist's shop amassed by members of a lively society based at Oxford House Adult Education Centre, Risca. *Open by appointment only.*

ST ASAPH

St Asaph Cathedral Treasury
The Cathedral, St Asaph, Clwyd (0745) 583429

Treasures of the Cathedral. *Open by appointment only.*

ST DAVIDS

Lleithyr Farm Museum
Whitesands Bay, Nr St Davids, Dyfed (0437) 720245

One of the many private farm museums in adapted outhouses showing the usual variety of agricultural implements, tractors and dairy and domestic utensils.

TREFECCA

The Howell Harris Museum
Trefecca, Brecon, Powys LD3 0PP (0874) 711423

An exhibition devoted to a leader of the 18th century Methodist Revival who also carried out experiments in economic and social planning in the village of Trefecca.

TRE'R-DDÔL

Amgueddfa'r Hen Gapel (Museum of Religious Life)
Tre'r-Ddôl, Nr Aberystwyth, Dyfed (097086) 407

A museum owned by the **National Museum of Wales** and operated by the Ceredigion District Council as a local museum and museum of religious life in Wales.

TYWYN

Narrow Gauge Railway Museum
Wharf Station, Tywyn, Gwynedd LL36 9EY (0654) 710472

An interpretation of the narrow gauge railway that operates as a tourist route but was once vital for transporting the slates of Abergynolwyn and Aberllefenni to the Cambrian railway at Tywyn.

WOLF'S CASTLE

Nant-y-Coy Mill
Tourist Centre and Museum, Wolf's Castle, Dyfed (0437) 87686

Another farm museum in an old mill house but with the addition of an exhibition of 200 jugs.

WOLVESNEWTON

The Model Farm Folk Collection
Wolversnewton, Nr Chepstow, Gwent NP6 6NZ (02915) 231

A collection of items of everyday life, mainly Victorian, housed in a late-18th-century barn.

WREXHAM

Erddig
Erddig Port, Wrexham, Clwyd LL13 0YT (0978) 355314

A National Trust house on the outskirts of Wrexham, fully restored and furnished, with much of 'downstairs' to see as well as 'upstairs'. Also contains an agricultural museum.

Geological Museum of North Wales
Bwlchgwyn Quarry, Nr Wrexham, Clwyd LL11 5UY (0978) 75753

A private museum containing a miscellany of geological and other specimens.

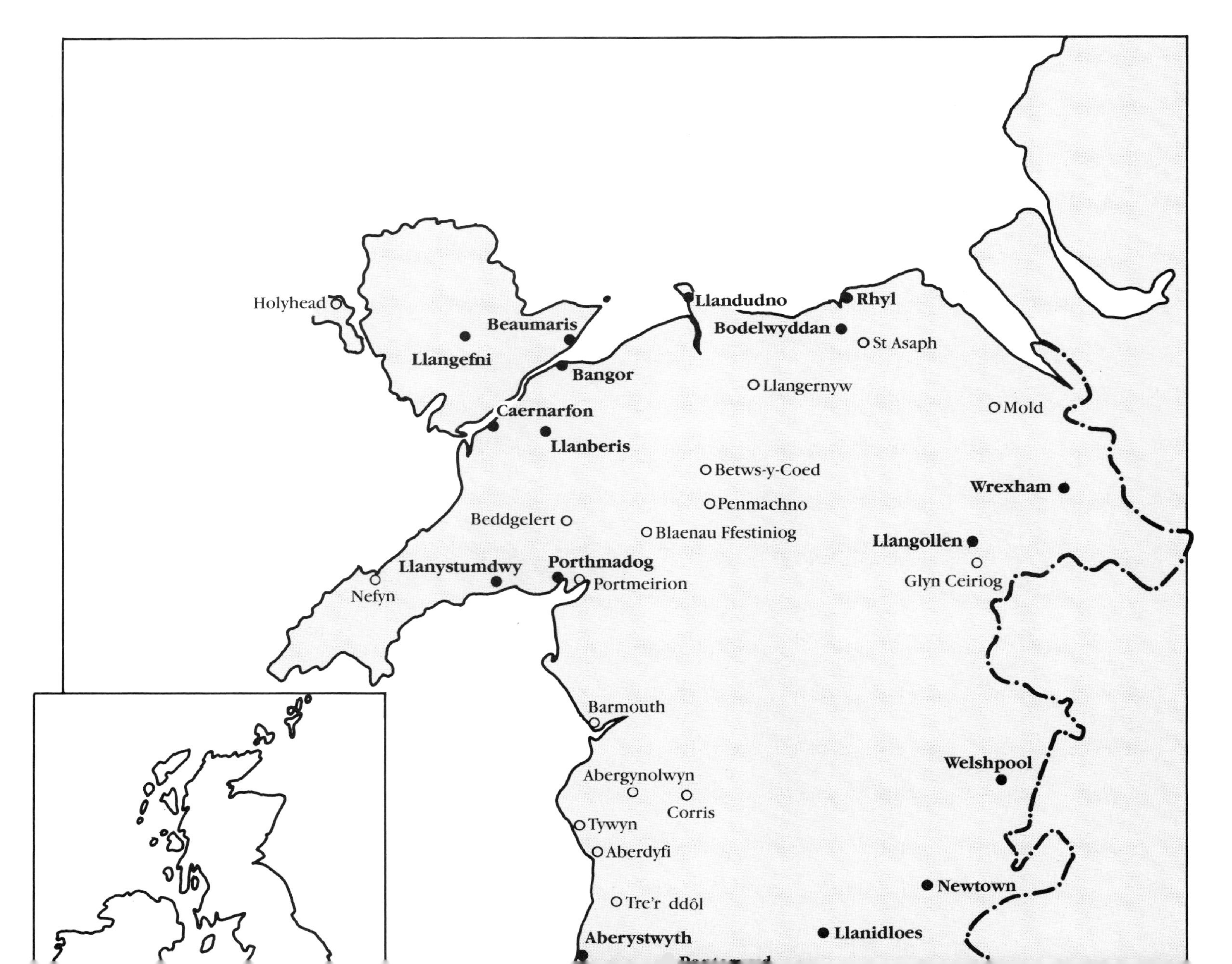
Holyhead
Beaumaris
Llangefni
Bangor
Caernarfon
Llanberis
Llandudno
Rhyl
Bodelwyddan
St Asaph
Llangernyw
Mold
Betws-y-Coed
Penmachno
Wrexham
Beddgelert
Blaenau Ffestiniog
Llangollen
Glyn Ceiriog
Llanystumdwy
Porthmadog
Portmeirion
Nefyn
Barmouth
Welshpool
Abergynolwyn
Corris
Tywyn
Aberdyfi
Newtown
Tre'r ddôl
Aberystwyth
Llanidloes

Rhaeadr
Llandrindod Wells
Trefecca
Brecon
Abergavenny
Blaenafon
Monmouth
Usk
Wolvesnewton
Chepstow
Caldicot
Pontypool
Caerleon
Newport
Risca
Rhymney Valley
Merthyr Tudful
Pontypridd
Trehafod
Cardiff
Penarth
Rhoose
Bridgend
Cynonville
Crynant
Neath
Margam
Porthcawl
Swansea
Pumsaint
Lampeter
Dre-Fach Felindre
Maesllyn
Glynarthen
Cynwyl Elfed
Carmarthen
Kidwelly
Llanelli
Llanddewi
Newcastle Emlyn
Cardigan
Laugharne
Tenby
Narberth
Clunderwen
Newport
Wolf's Castle
Haverfordwest
Pembroke
Mathry
Milford Haven
St Davids

Towns in which museums in this guide are located

● **Museums described**

○ Museums listed only (excluding town names already among museums described)

Index of Subjects

Index of Museum Names

Printed in the United Kingdom
for HMSO
Dd. 240100 C50 10/90 3735